BADMINTON

BADMINTON

Steven Boga

STACKPOLE BOOKS

Copyright © 1996 by Stackpole Books

Published by
STACKPOLE BOOKS
5067 Ritter Road
Mechanicsburg, PA 17055

Printed in the United States of America

10 9 8 7 6 5 4 3 2 1

First edition

Cover design by Caroline Miller with Tina Marie Hill

Library of Congress Cataloging-in-Publication Data

Boga, Steve, 1947–
    Badminton / Steven Boga.
        p.   cm.
    ISBN 0-8117-2487-5
    1. Badminton (Game)   I. Title
    GV1007.B64   1996
    796.34'5—dc20   95-22434
                                                 CIP

CONTENTS

INTRODUCTION

· ·

*"Ultimately, fitness and health are related
to everything we do, think, and feel."*
—George Leonard

Badminton. Quieter than bowling and stock-car racing, less
violent than football and boxing, and almost as fast as a
speeding bullet. It rewards power, reflexes, quickness, and intelligence. And it's only as competitive as you want to make it.

If it's a workout you want, badminton fits the bill. It's a faster
game than tennis, allowing players with even moderate skills to
maintain a heart rate sufficient for aerobic conditioning, while
burning 600 to 1,000 calories per hour. Play for an hour three
times a week, and you will see a marked decrease in body fat and
an increase in cardiovascular fitness. Plus, you'll have heaps of fun.

A study was done that measured the speed and
activity levels of badminton and tennis, with
astonishing results. Researchers compared a men's
singles tennis match between Bjorn Borg and John
McEnroe to a men's singles badminton match
between two Indonesians. The Borg-McEnroe match
lasted just over five hours, but the ball was in play—
and the players running—for only eighteen minutes
of the match. The badminton match lasted just over
two hours, but live action consumed one and a half
hours of that time. Moreover, the badminton players
changed directions up to twenty-nine times in a single rally, and six hundred to one thousand times in a
match.

The United States Badminton Association has a promotional video entitled "Badminton: Sports' Best Kept Secret," and ain't that the truth? Although thirteen million Americans reportedly play badminton at least once a week, top-flight badminton gets almost no news time. No reporters cover the badminton beat. The sport did get a boost in 1988, when it became an exhibition event at the Seoul Olympics, and again at the 1992 Olympics in Barcelona, when it became a full-medal sport. It was the first sport to sell out at Seoul, yet virtually no badminton action, live or taped, was beamed back to the United States from either Olympics. Badminton has a PR problem.

In Europe and Asia, on the other hand, badminton players get the attention and accolades accorded professional ballplayers in the United States. In Indonesia, top badminton players are financially secure for life, their pictures appear on giant billboards, and kids clamor for their autographs. Before the Barcelona Olympics, twenty-one thousand spectators attended a preliminary badminton match in Malaysia.

In Malaysia, where badminton is something of a religion, irate fans have been known to throw objects on the court during matches. Extra security is sometimes required for players. And it's not uncommon for spectators to take two shirts—light and dark—to matches. Because background is so important in badminton, with its white, darting shuttle, the fans (short for fanatics) don the dark shirts when their favorite player is facing them, and the light shirts when the opponent is facing them.

As an indication of how different it is in the United States, *Sports Illustrated's Sports Almanac* appears to have records and statistics from just about every sport—except badminton! Want to know the slow-pitch softball champs of 1981? How about the women's national archery champion of 1879? (Mrs. S. Brown, in case you didn't know.) Year-by-year champions are listed for chess, squash, lacrosse, fishing, and rodeo. You can even find curling results.

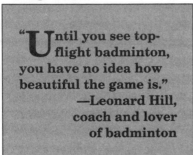

"**Until you see top-flight badminton, you have no idea how beautiful the game is.**"
—**Leonard Hill, coach and lover of badminton**

My first thought was that badminton is virtually ignored because it's a poor TV sport. With shuttle speeds up to 200 miles per hour, I reasoned, the sport must not adapt well to television.

Not so. Poring over video-tapes of several top-flight matches, I saw that the power and quickness of the sport transfers well to the 19-inch screen. Cameras placed above the action can capture much of the exhilaration and intensity of a badminton match. It succeeds at least as well as tennis, a sport that's enjoyed huge success on television.

I'm afraid that Andre Agassi has it right on this one: "Image is everything." And badminton's image for so many people—especially men—is of a dainty sport. But nothing could be further from the truth.

RULES

In the chapters that follow, you will learn about badminton strategy and technique. Before you can make sense of that, however, you have to understand the basics of play.

The complete rules of badminton are given in chapter 8, but here are the basics of the game:

Badminton is a racket sport for two or four players. As in tennis, two play singles, four play doubles.

The first serve of the game is from the right half court to the half diagonally opposite. If the receiving side commits a fault, the serving side gains a point and continues to serve. If the serving side commits a fault, no point is scored. In singles, the serve shifts to the opponent; in doubles, one partner serves until his side commits a fault, then his teammate serves. The exception: At the start of a doubles game, the serve shifts to the receiving team as soon as the serving side commits a fault.

In both singles and doubles, the serve is made alternately

from the right half and left half sides of the court, as in tennis. In doubles, the players on the receiving side do not shift half courts between serves.

Opponents change court ends after each game. The winning side serves first. In doubles, either partner may serve first and either opponent may receive first. The winner is the first side to win two games. If a third game is necessary, opponents change court ends again when one score reaches 8 in a game to 15, or 6 in a game to 11.

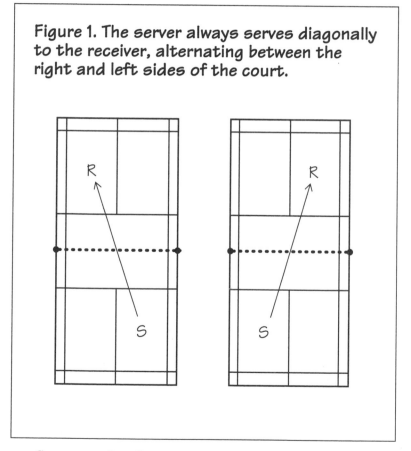

Figure 1. The server always serves diagonally to the receiver, alternating between the right and left sides of the court.

Games are played to 15 in men's singles and all doubles, and to 11 in women's singles. In a 15–point game, if the game is tied at 13–13, the side that first reached 13 has the option of extending it to 18 points. If this option is declined, the game may be set at 17 points when the score reaches 14–all. In women's singles, the game may be extended to 12 points if the score becomes 9–all or 10–all.

A one-game match, usually to 21, can be extended to 24 at 19–all and to 23 if tied at 20. Extending a game is a strategic decision that sometimes gives the player receiving serve a chance to come back and win.

The main faults in badminton occur in the following ways:

1. The server a) strikes the shuttle at a point higher than his waist, b) holds the racket head higher than his hand, or c) fails to serve the shuttle in the proper court.
2. The shuttle a) passes through or under the net, b) lands out of bounds, c) hits the ceiling or side walls, or d) touches the clothing or body of a player.

STROKES

The basic strokes are the serve, clear, drive, drop, and smash. The clear is a shot deep into the opponent's court. The drive is a fast shot hit with the racket about hip height. The drop is a finesse shot that causes the bird to fall near the net. The smash is a high-speed overhead shot. Clears, drives, and drops may be used on service.

● ● ● ● ● ●

My everlasting gratitude to the people everywhere who love this game and made this book possible. Special thanks to the accomplished players and coaches who gave generously of their time, especially Leonard Hill, Mike Walker, Sunny Kim, and Russ and Meiling Okuno.

Thanks also to the staff at the U.S. Badminton Association. Director Jim Hadley, Kate Spence, Barbara Juba, and others always came through when I needed them.

HISTORY

The deep roots of badminton are poorly defined. Some historians argue that it derives from a game called *battledore*, which was played in ancient China with two wooden paddles and a ball.

England's royal court records date the game to the twelfth century. But its more direct lineage is from a game in India known as *Poona* (after the Indian town of origin), which British soldiers took back to England around 1873.

When a group of such soldiers demonstrated the game to the eighth duke of Beaufort and his guests at the duke's country estate, called Badminton, it was a real catalyst. The duke took to the game in a big way, and for a time it was called "that game at Badminton," until it was inevitably shortened.

Soldiers returning to England from the colonial army introduced the game to other communities, such as Bath, Folkestone, Southsea, and Southampton, and even to the suburbs of London.

Badminton in Victorian England was quite the formal affair. Players wore Prince Albert coats, button shoes, chokers, and silk toppers. At least one club dropped a player for daring to remove his coat during a match.

Early courts were not rectangular but waisted, or hourglass shaped. They were typically 4 feet wider at the baselines than at the net. Apparently, this was because the game was played in large Victorian drawing rooms that featured massive doors opening into midcourt.

Shuttlecocks, all handmade, varied considerably in weight. Most rackets were made in France, where the sport had barely caught on. Singles and doubles were played, but it was also not uncommon to have three, four, or five players on a side, as in volleyball.

Many women were enthusiastic about badminton, although

Victorian propriety precluded their giving maximum effort. Men took to calling their style of play "hit and scream."

Badminton was introduced to the United States in 1878. The Badminton Club of the City of New York was formed that year, but its focus was more social than athletic. The club provided a weekend meeting for New York's society leaders. Names such as Astor, Roosevelt, Rockefeller, and Vanderbilt regularly appeared on the membership list. For twenty-five years after its inception, the club was a leading social rendezvous spot in New York.

One newspaper of the day described badminton in terms that would foreshadow its image today: "an easygoing game that does not require the muscular exertion demanded in bowling and is quite jolly withal."

Indeed, the weekend games at the New York club resembled a carnival as much as an athletic event. Different colored shuttles were used on nine courts shared by 150 members on a single afternoon. Pennants of red and gold, the club colors, decorated the poles that supported the nets. While resting between matches, players snacked on tea, cake, and sandwiches. Men wore tuxedos, Prince Albert coats, and dancing shoes. Women wore the long dresses in vogue during the Victorian era.

The net varied in height from 5 $\frac{1}{2}$ to 6 feet (5 feet today), making smashes and drops less effective. Shuttles, usually made with chicken feathers, varied in size, depending on the wishes of the players. Rackets were heavy, wooden implements resembling the tennis rackets of that time.

In 1887, the Bath Badminton Club of England codified the rules. Today those regulations, with modifications, continue to govern badminton all over the world.

The early twentieth century saw an increase in athleticism, a trend that spilled over into badminton clubs. After the scandal that erupted when Lyle Mahan took off his tuxedo coat during play, dress codes were relaxed. Men took off their coats, rolled up their sleeves, and began to sweat ever so slightly.

The standard English rules were adopted in the United States in 1905, and play improved simply because players knew what to expect: a standard shuttlecock, a rectangular court—44 by 20 feet for doubles, 44 by 17 feet for singles—and a net 5 feet high. Other rule changes encouraged a more physically demanding style of play.

For a long time, interest in badminton lagged in the United States. After World War I, American and Canadian soldiers returning from duty in England rekindled an enthusiasm for the game back home. A team from the English Badminton Association toured Canada in 1925 and 1930, sparking a veritable badminton renaissance. The game was touted as an elixir for what ailed you. Weight loss, muscle tone, on-the-job efficiency, and lower blood pressure were only some of the alleged benefits.

The Great Depression years of the thirties saw an increased emphasis on recreation. More leisure time meant more badminton time, and for a while it enjoyed a reputation as the fastest growing sport in America. Schools, YMCAs, and hundreds of newly formed clubs offered badminton instruction. Badminton became so popular in the thirties that a New York beauty salon installed a court atop its roof so that customers could exercise while their hair was setting.

When the game was taken up by movie stars and professional athletes from other sports, it generated even greater interest. Some of the Hollywood personalities who played were Sonja Henie, James Cagney, Pat O'Brien, Johnny Weissmuller, Boris Karloff, Andy Devine, Dick Powell, Harold Lloyd, Ginger Rogers, Loretta Young, Claudette Colbert, and Bette Davis. Joan Crawford was said to be so addicted to badminton that she would play on rainy days in a bathing suit. Douglas Fairbanks invented slightly different equipment for windy days, calling his modified game "Doug."

More interest in badminton meant better players, the best of whom drew large crowds. Even the erudite *Literary Digest* reported on matches. In the November 21, 1936, issue, readers learned that "last week the largest gallery that has ever seen a badminton match in New York City watched two players bat a ridiculous looking object back and forth across a five foot net. Stroking the bird furiously off the forehand and backhand, dribbling delicate drop shots over the net, Purcell and Davidson had the gallery constantly agog."

In 1936 Jess Willard and Bill Hurley toured the country, performing a series of badminton exhibitions during intermissions at movie houses. After one Willard-Hurley match at the Paramount in Los Angeles, the manager of the theater wrote, "To think that in a 3400 seat deluxe motion picture theater, a rapidly growing sport would so hold the interest of patrons that not a single person left their seat during the Badminton Game—a period of ten to twelve minutes—at neither [sic] of the four to five shows daily."

One of England's great players, Ken Davidson, came to the United States and soon became a great promoter of badminton. Until 1943 he teamed with Thelma Kingsbury and Hugh Forgie, traveling around the country staging badminton comedy shows. One reporter described the Davidson-Forgie antics thus: "You don't believe half the things you see . . . the act is built around the terrific power hitting of Forgie and the tricky finesse of Davidson . . . both tear around the court like junior blitzkriegs. Davidson's placements are uncanny; Forgie's recoveries unbelievable."

The Davidson-Forgie act became such a draw that they played in what was then the largest theater in the world: Radio City Music Hall. In England, they treated King George and Queen Elizabeth to a command performance.

After Davidson's death in 1954, the American Badminton Association established an annual award in his honor to go to the U.S. player who excelled in performance, sportsmanship, and contributions to the game. Hugh Forgie went on to entertain millions all over the world with his comedy show "Badminton on Ice."

The tremendous growth of badminton created a demand for a governing body. The International Badminton Federation was formed in 1934, and soon thereafter national championships were held in nine countries: Australia, Denmark, India, Malaya, Mexico, the Netherlands, Norway, Sweden, and the United States. By the mid-sixties, forty countries had joined the federation, and today more than fifty countries are members.

The American Badminton Association was founded in 1936, and the first national championships were held the following year in Chicago. Five thousand socialites in evening dress showed up to see the final rounds, the largest audience ever for a badminton match on the continent.

World War II stunted the growth of badminton. Many key players were called to war, armories closed their facilities to recreation, shuttles were hard to find, and West Coast blackouts eliminated night play.

But the sport bounced back in the fifties, the glory years for U.S. badminton. The 1952 U.S. men's team finished second to

Malaya for the Thomas Cup, and American women were the best in the world.

International teams compete every three years for both the men's and women's titles. The men's trophy was donated in 1940 by George A. Thomas, president of the International Badminton Federation, but World War II and its aftermath delayed matches for the trophy until 1949. The first three Thomas Cups were won by Malaya, the next three by Indonesia. No non-Asian country has ever won the men's competition.

In 1956 Mrs. H. S. Uber, a British badminton star, contributed a trophy for international women's competition. Led by Judith Devlin Hashman, the U.S. women won the first three Uber Cups, the last in 1963. A former Baltimore schoolteacher, Hashman played world-class badminton between 1954 and 1967. During those thirteen years, she won thirty-two U.S. championships—twelve in singles, twelve in doubles (ten with her sister, Sue Devlin Peard), and eight in mixed doubles—and ten All-England (unofficial world championship) titles. Since her retirement, Japan, China, and Indonesia have dominated the women's competition.

United States badminton in the 1990s flourishes in schools and colleges, where it does especially well as an intramural sport. In high schools, interschool competition is more common for girls than for boys, which tarnishes its image in the eyes of males. Inexpensive, nonviolent, and requiring a challenging mix of agility and power, badminton deserves a better fate.

The American Badminton Association is now the United States Badminton Association, an organization that supervises local, state, and regional tournaments and conducts national and junior national championships annually.

With the variety of big-money sports available in the United

States, passion for badminton here will never reach the obsession level it has in Europe and Asia. Some European and Asian cities have special badminton halls, where matches are often played before thousands of screaming, standing-room-only spectators. Copenhagen, for example, has twenty-two badminton halls, with four to twelve courts in each. In Asia, badminton teams are heavily subsidized by the government, and players become national heroes. More than twenty-one thousand fans attended an Olympic qualifier match in Malaysia.

In the United States, there are good players but no dominant players on the world stage. The best Americans are not in the top one hundred in the world.

To excel in badminton, you have to love the game. There is no six-figure prize money for tournament winners, no million-dollar sneaker contracts. "Reebok offered to give me one pair of shoes to wear at the Olympics," said Joy Kitzmiller, former U.S. badminton champion and one of three female badminton players who represented the United States at Barcelona.

BADMINTON TIME LINE

1873 Game introduced in England and called *badminton*.
1873 First badminton club formed in Bath, England.
1878 First U.S. badminton club formed.
1890s Game introduced in Canada and the United States.
1895 National Badminton Association formed in the United States.
1899 First All-England Championship for men.
1900 First Women's Championships.
1931 Canadian Badminton Association founded.
1934 International Badminton Federation founded.
1936 American Badminton Federation founded.
1937 First United States Championships.
1948 Thomas Cup, triennial international competition for men, established.
1957 Uber Cup, triennial international competition for women, established.

COURT AND EQUIPMENT

Badminton is refreshingly simple. All you really need is a racket, a bird, and a net. No net? Just tie string or rope between two objects. No set boundaries or yardstick? Just step off a court and throw down some shirts for markers. Badminton is right at home both indoors and out. The main problem with playing indoors is that very few houses built in the past fifty years feature 1,000-square-foot rooms with 30-foot-high ceilings. The main problem outdoors is wind.

You can enjoy yourself with just racket and bird. If you have a gentle prevailing wind, plenty of open space, and no partner, you can make a game out of smashing the bird into the wind, running to where it comes down, and smashing it again. See how long you can keep the bird aloft.

COURT

Although an official badminton court is 20 feet wide (17 feet for singles) by 44 feet long (Fig. 2), don't feel you have to stand on ceremony. The backyard game can be played on a court of almost any size and shape. In Victorian England, birthplace of the modern game, badminton was played on an hourglass-shaped court, so the game will certainly accommodate an ill-placed rhododendron.

In doubles, each service court is 2 feet 6 inches shorter than in singles but 1 foot 6 inches wider. Once the bird is in play, the baseline is the same for both games, but each sideline in doubles extends 1 foot 6 inches beyond the singles sideline.

Figure 2a. The standard singles court.

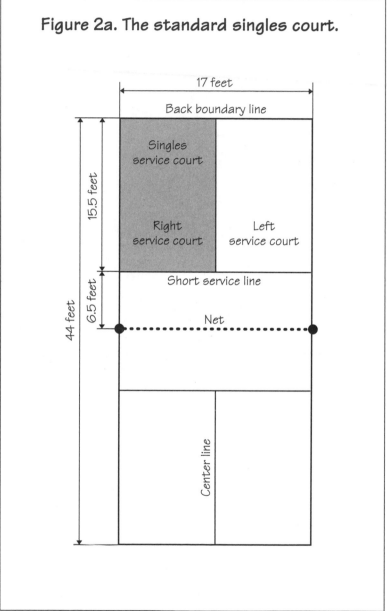

Figure 2b. The standard doubles court.

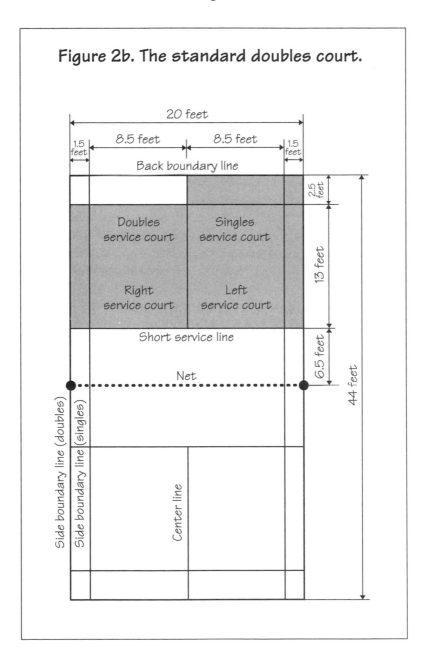

No matter what size court you use, try to maintain at least 2 feet of clearance on the sides of the court and at least 4 feet at each end. National and international competition requires a height of more than 30 feet, and you would be wise to allow almost that much for local matches, as a lower ceiling will restrict serves and clears.

The court lines, officially 1 $^1/_2$ inches wide, are best painted in white on a dark, nonreflecting floor. For temporary lines, try white water-base paint or masking tape.

A net 5 feet 1 inch in height bisects the court. The net posts are placed on the doubles sideline, and the net dips in the center to a height of exactly 5 feet.

Lighting

Your objective with lighting is to assure that the shuttle, regardless of flight path, stands out like a white dove, without the light blinding the players.

Ideally, the only light fixtures should be alongside both sides of the court near the net, approximately 12 to 16 feet above the floor, depending on the height of the ceiling and any reflection from it. The lights should be outside the boundary lines so as not to interfere with play. Ceiling lights over the court and background wall lights will tend to blind players as they follow the flight of the shuttle.

One way to arrange appropriate lighting is to build a 10-foot extension on each net post and top it with a bulb, 750 watts or stronger, sticking straight up. Use no reflectors. Better yet, add a horizontal crosspiece near the top, allowing it to extend 3 feet on each side of the net, and place downward-pointing 500-watt bulbs at both ends of the crosspiece. To diffuse the light, you can drape the bulbs with a white translucent material.

EQUIPMENT

Shuttle

Variously called a *shuttlecock, bird, birdie,* or "that damn thing," a shuttle cannot be mistaken for anything else. A shuttle is either feathered or plastic (Fig. 3). If feathered, it is made of cork, goatskin, thread, and sixteen carefully selected goose feathers. To outfit one shuttle, it takes a whole goose to supply enough quality feathers, not to mention part of a goat, so treat your bird with due respect. Feathered birds arriving fresh from the factory have the proper amount of moisture already in the feathers; if not abused, they will survive a lot of play without breaking up.

Proper care of shuttles, especially the feathered ones, will extend their life. Feathered shuttles come in tubes with instructions on the humidity necessary to keep them from drying out and cracking. Their greatest enemy is hot, dry air. Manufacturers try to preserve the moisture by treating the tubes containing the shuttles. Keep your shuttles in a cool, moist place, 60 to 65 degrees Fahrenheit. Humidity of 70 to 80 percent is ideal. Avoid any action that would damage feathers. If a feather becomes ruffled, smooth it. Although synthetic outdoor shuttles are more durable, care should still be taken to protect them from prolonged exposure to the elements.

Figure 3. Plastic birds (left) are probably best for beginners; feathered shuttles (right) require a bit more care.

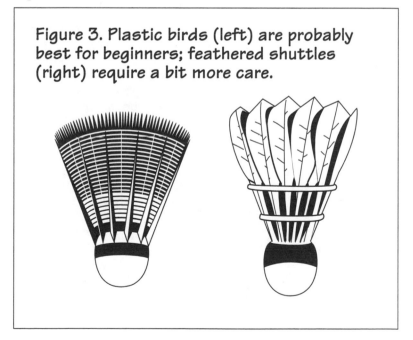

The rules of badminton used to specify that feathered shuttles must weigh between 73 and 85 grains. But no one knew what a grain was (15.432 grains to a gram), so now Law 4.2 says that "the shuttle shall weigh from 4.74 to 5.50 grams." It's still about $\frac{1}{6}$ ounce. Backyard shuttles, with a synthetic skirt and rubber tip, weigh 100 to 110 grains, or a hefty $\frac{1}{4}$ ounce. In either case, shuttles are extremely light, making them susceptible to the vagaries of moving air. If you play outside, wind adds a daunting, sometimes amusing challenge that is more or less the same for both sides. Change sides often, and hold on to your sense of humor.

Feathered shuttles are marked by weight or designated slow, medium, or fast. The main factors that determine the speed of a shuttle are the air temperature, the shuttle's weight, and the shape of the ends of the feathers. The warmer the room, the faster the shuttle. The average weight of a pointed-end feathered shuttle in a heated room is 76 grains and a rounded-end 79 grains. A pointed-end feathered shuttle will fly farther than a rounded-end of the same weight. Each grain of weight adds about 4 inches to the length of flight.

Here, right out of Law 4.4 of the USBA Official Rules of Play, is a shuttle test you can do yourself. A player of average strength stands behind the baseline and strikes the shuttle with a full underhand stroke that makes contact over the back boundary line. The shuttle, hit at an upward angle and in a direction parallel to the sidelines, is considered properly paced if it falls not less than 1 foot 9 inches or more than 3 feet 3 inches short of the other back boundary line (Fig. 4).

Racket

The rules of badminton place no restrictions on the length or weight of the racket. Manufacturers have arrived at a standard weight of 4 $\frac{1}{2}$ to 5 $\frac{1}{2}$ ounces and a length of 26 inches. The length usually breaks down this way: head, 10 inches; shaft, 11 inches; and grip, 5 inches. The balance point is the midpoint, 13 inches from either end.

Rackets used to be made entirely of wood, but now backyard models are all metal with tempered steel shafts, colored nylon strings, and PVC grips. Metal rackets eliminate the need for a press, as they will not warp like wooden frames.

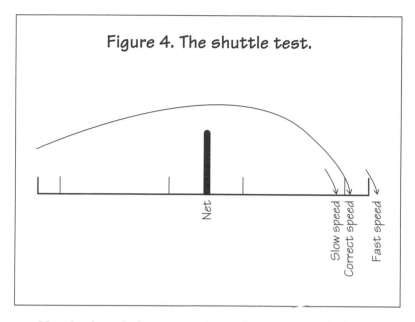

Figure 4. The shuttle test.

Net

Slow speed
Correct speed
Fast speed

Most backyard players acquire rackets as part of a larger set that includes net and birds. But the racket is the most important piece of badminton equipment, so you may want to order a quality racket separately. Prices vary from $10 to $120.

When selecting a racket, pay particular attention to the size of the handle. It should fit snugly and feel right when you swing. An average handle is $3\,^3/_4$ inches in circumference. If the handle is too small for your grip, you can build it up with a gauze wrap; if it is too big, you need a different racket.

You can save time and money by learning to repair your own broken strings. All you need is some gut, which can be salvaged from old rackets, and a couple of awls, of the type on a Swiss army knife. Study the way the knots are tied on your racket and practice once or twice, and all will become clear. If, however, a full restringing job is indicated, take your racket to a professional stringer.

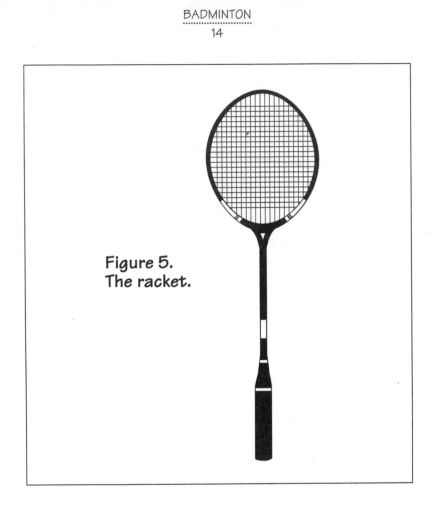

Figure 5.
The racket.

Net

The net should be made of all-weather mesh with sleeves and reinforcing tape top and bottom. Look for easy setup that doesn't require digging holes. Forster Manufacturing Company in Wilton, Maine, makes badminton sets that include a 20-by-2-foot, sleeved, six-ply, polyethylene mesh net with top and bottom tapes. It can be firmly stretched from post to post.

	Official Badminton	Backyard Badminton
Shuttle	16 goose feathers, cork covered with goatskin	plastic
Racket	graphite, ceramic, or boron; gut strings	wood or aluminum
Venue	indoors	outdoors
Shuttle speed	up to 200 mph	more leisurely
Dress	75 percent of outfit must be white	casual, anything goes

GRIP, POSITION, AND FOOTWORK

···

GRIP

The two basic badminton grips—forehand and backhand—are the same as their tennis counterparts. You will use the forehand grip for strokes made overhead or on the right side of the body, and backhand for strokes made on the left side of the body. (If you are left-handed, reverse the above and just about everything else in this chapter.)

Begin by grasping the throat of the racket with the left hand. Turn the racket so that its face is perpendicular to the playing surface. With the right hand, shake hands with the racket, closing the thumb around the grip so that the side of the thumb rests on the back bevel. Position the hand at the end of the grip to gain optimum wrist action. Grip the racket firmly with the fingers (not the palm) for power shots, looser for finesse shots. In either case, the fingers, especially the forefinger and third finger, are comfortably spread.

The point of the V formed by thumb and forefinger should point at the top bevel of the eight-sided handle. In order to find your comfort zone, you may move your hand along the grip or spread and close your fingers, but don't change the position of this V.

To achieve a backhand grip, slide the hand counterclockwise until the V is on the top left bevel. It's important to place your thumbprint against the back bevel of the handle. This thumb position lends needed support for quick drives and deep clears.

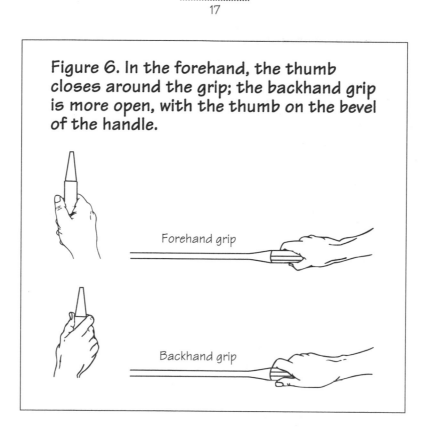

Figure 6. In the forehand, the thumb closes around the grip; the backhand grip is more open, with the thumb on the bevel of the handle.

Forehand grip

Backhand grip

COURT POSITION

Call it the *playing position, center position, basic position, or ready position*—whatever you call it, get used to finding it as often as possible. Equidistant from the net and baseline, midway between the sidelines, it's the spot on the court from which you can best reach the most shots. Depending on your particular strengths and weaknesses, you may want to adjust slightly. Most players will play somewhat left of center to feature a stronger forehand over a weaker backhand.

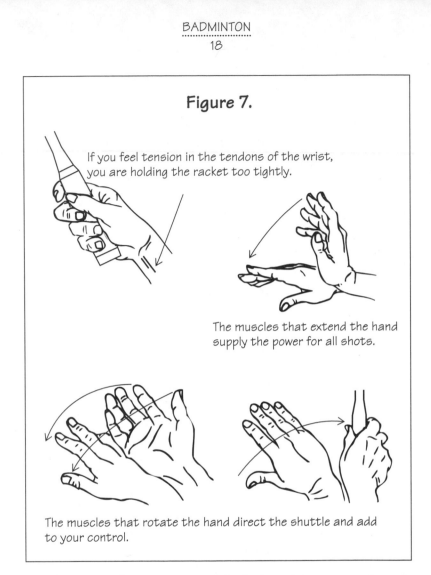

Figure 7.

If you feel tension in the tendons of the wrist, you are holding the racket too tightly.

The muscles that extend the hand supply the power for all shots.

The muscles that rotate the hand direct the shuttle and add to your control.

To prepare for your opponent's shots, get to your ready position (Fig. 8) and stand alertly, knees slightly bent, feet spread about shoulder width, weight evenly distributed on the balls of both feet. You should be balanced, relaxed, and ready for quick action, which, in badminton, is never far away.

The racket should be held in front of the body, with the wrist and grip about waist level and the racket head near shoulder height. Players vary the racket position slightly to suit their own style; experiment to find what is comfortable for you.

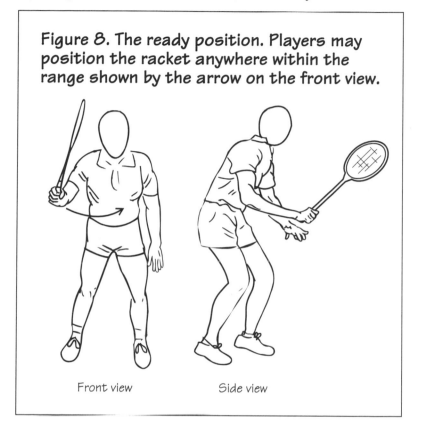

Figure 8. The ready position. Players may position the racket anywhere within the range shown by the arrow on the front view.

Front view   Side view

Keep your eyes focused on the shuttle from the time it leaves your opponent's racket. Your goal is to calculate direction as quickly as possible and move your feet in response. The shuttle usually comes so swiftly that there is no time to survey the court, to consciously think about what you will do next. Instead, badminton places a premium on instincts and reflexes. Points are often scored because one player lacks the reflexes necessary to move feet or racket into position quickly enough to return the shuttle.

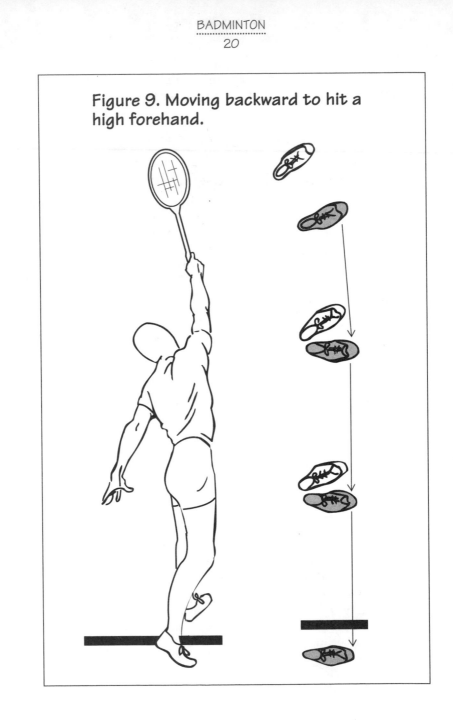

Figure 9. Moving backward to hit a high forehand.

FOOTWORK

Capable opponents will try to move the shuttle—and hence you—around the court. To move quickly enough to reach the shuttle and still have time for the stroke, proper footwork is essential. You may have good eye-racket coordination and great strokes, but they will be ineffective if you can't get into position.

The best beginning is an alert ready position. Keep the body ready to move in any direction by flexing the knees slightly and staying on the balls of both feet.

Running forward toward the net is the most natural movement and thus the easiest type of footwork to practice. Moving backward, on the other hand, is not at all natural. Unless you are used to playing quarterback in the T formation, you may find backpedaling toward the baseline uncomfortable. Practice the skill.

To move back to the baseline, keep the feet close to the court and skip or bounce backward (Fig. 9). To hit an overhead or forehand stroke in the deep right court, lead with the right foot and skip diagonally back to your right. Finish with the left side turned slightly toward the net and the left foot forward. Be sure to go back far enough to position your body behind the falling shuttle. That will allow you to transfer your body weight forward onto your left foot, adding power to the stroke.

To play a deep backhand, lead with the left foot and skip diagonally back. When you're ready to stroke, the right foot should be diagonally forward and the right side toward the net.

Like a quarterback, a retreating badminton player should keep head and eyes forward at all times. If you have to turn your back to the net and run with your head down, you probably won't have time to turn back and hit the bird.

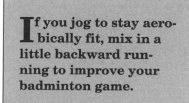

If you jog to stay aerobically fit, mix in a little backward running to improve your badminton game.

Short steps at the beginning of a run toward the shuttle will give you a quicker start. A well-balanced hitting stance not only improves the execution of your shots, but also leads to a quicker getaway for the next shot. When more than one step is required to reach the shuttle, make the last step the longest.

Sometimes, when an extra few inches are needed to reach a forehand shot in the forecourt, it can be obtained by stretching out the right foot ahead of the left foot. This technique should be used only for close net play; when greater force is needed, make sure the left foot is forward.

SHOTS

···

There are two basic ways to hit a shuttle: forehand and back-hand. You will rely on the forehand when the shuttle is hit to your right or above your head, and the backhand when it's hit to your left (left-handers reverse this).

To be successful in badminton, you must have a flexible wrist and be adept at both forehand *and* backhand. Unlike tennis, bad-minton is very much a wrist game. A well-timed whip of the wrist supplies explosive power to a badminton stroke. It is wrist snap that enables you to clear a bird from baseline to baseline. It is the last-minute flick of the wrist that lends deception to your shots.

Figure 10. The last 3 feet of the racket's forward motion determine power, speed, control, and deception.

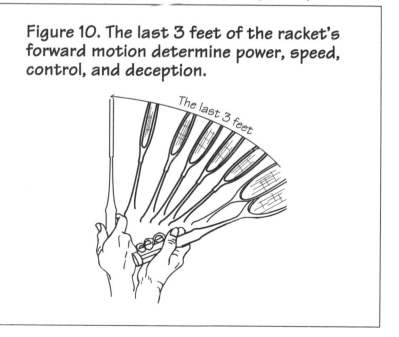

Proper wrist action is vital to success in badminton, as it is in baseball. In fact, if you grew up batting and throwing, you are already tuned in to the wrist snap that badminton demands. Some coaches tell their players to imagine they are throwing the head of the racket at the shuttle. Others have them imagine their wrist bending like that of a house painter wielding a brush.

Improve your wrist snap with this drill: Press your upper arm and elbow tight to your body, and stroke using only your wrist. When you feel comfortable with the movement and timing of the wrist, return to full strokes. If at any point you feel you aren't getting enough wrist action, try loosening your grip between shots, then tightening it at contact.

The striking of the shuttle can be broken down into three phases: 1) the backswing; 2) the forward swing (and hit); and 3) the follow-through. These phases can be thought of as 1) preparing to hit the shuttle; 2) hitting the shuttle; and 3) finishing hitting the shuttle.

Regardless of which stroke is used, the shuttle should be hit as early and as high as possible, especially when the bird is close to the net. A shuttle should never be allowed to drop if it can be reached higher in its arc. Meeting the shuttle early enables you to make crisp, controlled hits, which in turn gives your opponent less time to reach the shuttle. Conversely, late hitting not only causes improper stroking, but also allows an opponent more time to make his return. It's important to remember that any shot that can be contacted above net level is potentially an offensive shot, and any shot contacted below the net is almost certainly defensive.

FOREHAND

The stroke you will use most often is the overhead version of the forehand. As with all strokes, the overhead arm swing can be divided into backswing and forward swing. There should be a slight pause between the two.

When you have enough time, draw the racket back early, then bend your elbow and cock your wrist. That should drop the racket head to near shoulder height. Pause for a moment. Then, as your arm swings forward, keep your wrist in its cocked position. Your elbow straightens, but your wrist remains cocked.

At the proper moment, whip the wrist forward, snapping through the shuttle. At the moment of contact, your arm and the racket shaft should form a perfectly straight line.

After the bird is struck, finish the stroke. Unless it is a quick defensive block, a thorough follow-through will add power to the stroke.

BACKHAND

Although you will no doubt favor your forehand, you must also develop an effective backhand. But don't try to do too much with it. Almost exclusively a defensive stroke, it is rarely hit for a winner.

Except for the occasional drop shot, most backhands should be hit high and deep. Deep shots take longer to reach, providing more time for you to set yourself for your own return. But it is difficult to backhand a bird a long distance. It takes perfect timing, which requires practice.

Imagine you're facing the net in the ready position, when the bird is hit to your left, about waist-high. Your response should be as follows:

1. Pivot on your left foot and swing your right foot around in front of your body; your right side is now facing the net.
2. As you move your feet, draw your racket into the backswing position. Imagine a coiling action as you turn your right shoulder. Your right hand should now be next to your left shoulder.
3. Shift your weight onto your left foot.
4. Now uncoil. As the right side of your body drives forward, your weight shifts to your right foot. You will notice that your elbow straightens as you swing.

5. Keep your wrist cocked until just before the hit. Snap the wrist to power the racket forward.
6. During the follow-through, if your wrist is properly relaxed, it will roll over slightly, turning the palm up.

TYPES OF SHOTS

Once you are able to execute basic forehands and backhands, you can concentrate on learning the four fundamental badminton shots: clear, drop, smash, and drive.

Clear

Analogous to the deep lob in tennis, the clear (Fig. 11) is the most common shot in badminton. Like the tennis lob, it can be offensive, moving an opponent back from the net, or defensive, gaining time to improve your position. Or perhaps it's the only shot possible.

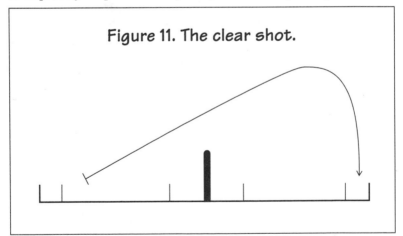

Figure 11. The clear shot.

The clear can be hit overhand or underhand, forehand or backhand, though backhand is difficult to accomplish. The clear appears easier than it is; against a capable player, it must be hit high and deep. Beginners are often satisfied with merely hitting the bird back with no real purpose. This is a mistake. When clearing, you should always target the bird to your opponent's baseline.

Badminton coach Leonard Hill says, "The first thing I was told twenty-seven years ago when I was learning the sport: You have to learn to hit a clear. That's not as easy as it sounds. It's forty-four feet from end to end. You have to have good technique and be fairly strong. If you hit it short, good players will put it someplace you can't reach."

Hit a clear high enough that your opponent can't possibly intercept it. A bird hit high plummets straight down at the end of its flight, making it more difficult to return and giving you more time to position yourself defensively.

The two most common mistakes with an overhead clear are as follows:

- Hitting with a bent arm.
- Contacting the shuttle behind the body.

Drop

The drop (Fig. 12) is a slow, gentle shot that falls just over the net into the opponent's forecourt. Although it sometimes wins a point, its main purpose is to force your opponent to hit from below net level, giving you an opportunity to follow with a smash. Because the drop travels so slowly, it must be hit as far as possible from the opponent and executed with deception. That means using the same grip, footwork, stance, and backswing as for the clear. If done properly, your opponent receives the message that a clear is coming. If it is obvious that you have hit a drop, the return will be easy for your opponent even if you have placed the bird perfectly in a front corner. On the other hand, do a good job of camouflaging the drop, and you may hit a winner even with marginal placement. If you force your opponent to scramble forward, lunge for the bird, and hit upward, you have stroked an effective drop shot.

To hit a drop, contact the bird as high in its flight as possible and far enough in front of you that your racket begins its downward arc at the moment of impact. This reduces the forward momentum you impart to the bird.

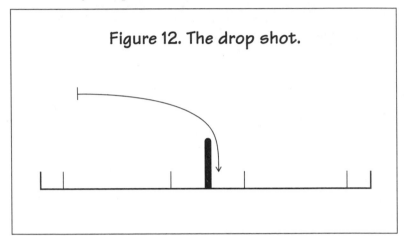

Figure 12. The drop shot.

What separates a drop from a clear is that just before contacting a drop shot, your wrist should be gently locked. With less wrist snap and a restrained backswing, the bird will travel a shorter distance. Of all the badminton shots, the drop requires the most delicate touch and the greatest wrist control.

The drop is an essential arrow in your quiver, because it is the only shot that is directed to the front corners near the net. The smash and drive are hit to the midcourt or deeper; the clear should always be placed in the backcourt. In order to move your opponent around the entire court, the drop shot must be part of your repertoire. It is particularly effective against a slow, weary, or out-of-shape opponent.

Body position for the overhead backhand drop shot is similar to the overhead backhand clear—right foot forward, body coiled so that your back is almost facing the net. The striking point is as high as you can comfortably reach and slightly in front of the right shoulder.

The following are some common drop shot mistakes:

- Incorrect angle of racket face.
- Incomplete follow-through—that is, tapping the shuttle.
- Facing the net instead of turning your back to it.

Smash

The smash (Fig. 13) is a powerful overhead shot used to put away a shuttle that is above the height of the net. As badminton's main point maker, it is a constant—and sometimes ill-advised—temptation, especially for beginners.

Struck from a point high above your head, the smash features greater racket speed than any other stroke. There is almost no defense against a good one. Moreover, a smash has great psychological value; the recipient of smash after smash can be engulfed by a tsunami of doom.

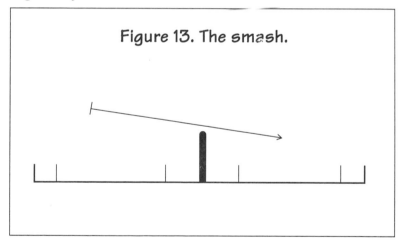

Figure 13. The smash.

Still, some players rely too heavily on the smash, to the point that it becomes predictable—and exhausting. Beginners are especially likely to be smash-happy, even when other shots are more appropriate. A player who smashes relentlessly is more likely to tire in the latter stages of a match. His shots will then be less powerful and accurate.

When you smash, your racket should catch the shuttle high and in front of you. It should travel as a downward-angled line drive and be aimed far to your opponent's backhand or, if you're very accurate, at his right hip. To slow your opponent's anticipation of your smash returns, mask them as clears or drops. Try to use the same grip, footwork, body position, backswing, and contact point as for your other shots.

The smash is probably most effective when struck from the short service line or closer, but accomplished players can gain an advantage with a smash from almost any court position.

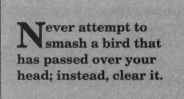

Never attempt to smash a bird that has passed over your head; instead, clear it.

In preparation for a smash, your body should be at a right angle to the net, with your left foot forward and left shoulder turned toward the net. As the bird descends, most of your weight rests on your right foot. The head of the racket is cocked behind your head and right shoulder, approximately horizontal to the playing surface. At the proper moment, determined by experience, your body starts to uncoil to the left, trunk and shoulders rotating forward. Your elbow is straightened, your right shoulder moves forward, and your weight is shifted from your right foot to your left. Your arm rises to full extension, and the bird is struck about 1 foot in front of your body. As the racket strikes the bird, with the full force of your arm, shoulder, and body behind it, your wrist snaps sharply forward, adding whipping power to the stroke. Beginners, however, should sacrifice power for timing.

Your mental image should be of covering the bird—that is, hitting down on it and following through toward the ground. The direction of the follow-through should be the same as the path of the bird.

Above all, you must watch the birdie. Concentrate on its path as it flies toward you and until after it has been struck by your racket. The forehand smash is very much a timing shot; the more of them you hit, the easier to gauge when you should swing.

Reviewing the basic components of the forehand smash, your arm should be fully extended when your racket meets the bird;

the right side of your body should be driving forward to help power the stroke; your wrist should uncock at the proper moment to provide further power; and you must watch the bird to assure proper timing and accuracy.

Some common faults when hitting the forehand smash are as follows:

- Hitting it too flat. A bird hit far out into your opponent's court is easier to retrieve.
- Hitting with a bent elbow instead of a fully extended arm. This makes for a flat shot rather than a steep one.
- Hitting while moving backward.
- Moving into position too late. This usually means hitting off balance or without your whole body behind the shot.
- Jumping to hit a smash. This is okay for experts, but beginners should avoid it. It's tiring, and the variation in height at which the bird is taken makes consistency hard to achieve.

Some players find that they gain balance and accuracy by raising the left arm just prior to the stroke, virtually pointing at the bird. The arm is lowered naturally as the body turns and the racket is brought up and over the bird.

Many players, even some beginners, can hit a forehand smash when the shuttle is high, short, and overhead or slightly to the right. After all, that stroke is similar to an overhand throw. But what if it's to the left? A backhand smash is an advanced technique, one that even accomplished players often fail to hit with great power. It then becomes necessary to rely heavily on deception and accurate placement.

If the shuttle is high and only slightly to the left, you can use one of three shots: backhand smash, backhand drive, or round-the-head smash (Fig. 14). This last, if done properly, is the strongest shot. It uses the forehand grip and is similar to the forehand smash, but you stand more squarely to the net than for the conventional smash, and bend your upper body sideways left as your arm comes through. Your weight rests mainly on the left foot. With your elbow sharply bent, the racket travels back well behind your head, then sweeps around it, your forearm brushing the top of your head before straightening. In this way, the potential for a severe wrist snap, and therefore a powerful shot, is great.

Because the smash comes fairly naturally, we tend to under-emphasize it in practice. Yet, just as with other shots, there are a lot of things that can break down. If you have trouble with your smashes, stay with the basics.

Figure 14. The round-the-head shot.

Drive

The drive (Fig. 15) is a line-drive shot that travels parallel to the ground, passing close over the net. Usually struck at or below waist level, it is a primary weapon in mixed doubles, where it is used to keep the male moving from side to side. It should be used sparingly in singles.

To generate the power necessary for an effective forehand drive, your left foot must be placed forward of the right. As the racket is pulled back in preparation for the shot, with your elbow bent and wrist cocked, your body coils so that your back turns toward the net. Both knees are slightly bent, with most of your weight on the rear foot.

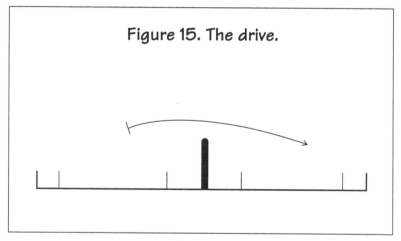

Figure 15. The drive.

As the bird approaches, the racket rushes to meet it. Your elbow straightens for the shot, your body pivots, and your weight is transferred from the rear to the front foot. Just as the bird is struck—ideally about 1 foot in front of your body—your wrist sharply uncocks. The follow-through is in line with the flight of the bird, leaving you facing the net and ready for your opponent's return.

The following are some common drive mistakes:

- Late racket preparation.
- Striking the bird after it has passed the body.

- Hitting the bird at less than peak speed.
- Hitting with an upward trajectory.

Air resistance affects the flight of shuttlecocks more than it does the balls used in many other sports, and that takes some adjustment. Even though a shuttle can reach dazzling speeds, it falls more slowly than a tennis ball and doesn't follow the same parabolic path. This causes many a beginner to swing too early. Like a hitter facing a junk-ball pitcher, you have to wait. Practice to perfect your timing.

STRATEGY

· ·

In badminton, offense can change to defense and back again in the bat of an eye—or two bats of a shuttlecock. A clear in response to a smash can drive the smasher back, forcing a weak, defensive reply. A delicate drop shot off a drive may cause the driver to scramble forward just to get a racket on the bird.

Badminton demands constant thinking. The successful player is forever planning, probing, and searching. Each shot has a purpose.

A basic beginner's strategy is to alternate clear and drop shots, adding drives and smashes as openings develop. Clears near the baseline mixed with drops near the net force your opponent into an enervating race for survival.

Try to put your opponent on the defensive. Respond to her clear with a drop shot, not another clear. If she meets your drop with another drop, then clear. If she then clears, respond with another drop, unless she is so close to the net that a clear is called for. In all cases, try to get back to center court after every shot.

Proper techniques will make it easier to return to base camp after each shot. Strive for good balance after each stroke. Have your momentum going toward center court. Hit clears, which afford you more time.

There are important strategic elements in badminton. If you're not convinced that strategy plays an important role, you will be after you're trounced by an experienced player with less athletic ability than you have. In other words, you will be beaten by someone who outthinks you on the court.

Even if you are inexperienced, you will benefit from

making *planned* moves rather than merely reacting to your opponent's shots. As soon as you are able to execute a basic clear, smash, and drop shot, you are ready to apply some simple strategy.

SINGLES STRATEGY

Since a singles player must cover the entire court, any successful offensive strategy seeks to make an opponent run, run, run. Move opponents around the court with a mix of clears, smashes, and drops. Hit to undefended spots. Playing against opponents of similar ability, you will not have to make perfect placements to be effective. As usual, practice will increase proficiency.

Intermediate singles players should make frequent use of the same three basic shots, albeit with greater accuracy, deception, and mix of speeds. Learn to use round-the-head shots in place of weak backhands; attacking clears in place of defensive ones; and enough deception to keep your opponent off-balance and unable to make adequate returns.

Serving

Serving (Fig. 16) in singles is critical for two reasons:

- The server has the first opportunity to err (Fig. 17).
- The player must hold serve to score.

The centerpiece of singles serving is the high, deep serve. Although the shuttle can be served to various areas of the service court, it is most effective when placed near the intersection of the back line and the center service line (Fig. 18). Such a placement reduces the possible return angles, forcing your opponent to hit his return near the center of your court.

A high, deep serve that lands a couple of inches inside the back line is the most valuable serving weapon in your arsenal. Still, watch the receiver's setup position for clues as to when a surprise serve may work. For example, if the receiver sets up deep in the court, you may want to mix in a short, low serve as a change of pace. A well-executed drop will begin to fall about the time it reaches the top of the net, making it impossible for your opponent to smash it downward. On the other hand, a low serve will be returned more quickly, giving the server less time to react.

Figure 16. The service: holding and dropping the shuttle; swinging the racket.

Figure 17. Common serve mistakes include dropping the shuttle too close to the body and contacting the shuttle too high.

If the receiver cheats to one side of the court, often to the left to feature a stronger forehand, hit a quick drive serve to the backhand side. If your opponent doesn't appear to react well, a drive serve hit right at him may also be effective.

Returning Serve

In singles, most serves are directed high and deep to the corners, forcing the returner to backpedal into position for an effective return.

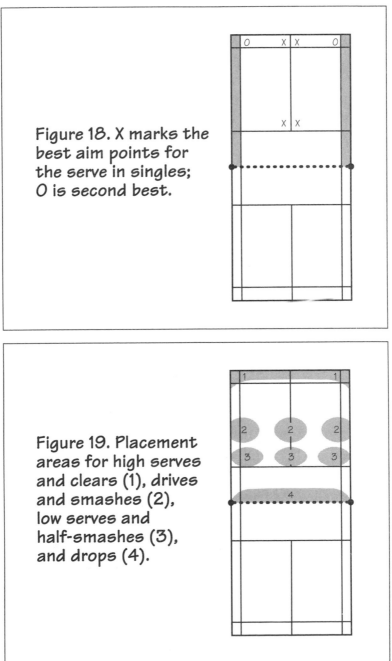

Figure 18. X marks the best aim points for the serve in singles; O is second best.

Figure 19. Placement areas for high serves and clears (1), drives and smashes (2), low serves and half-smashes (3), and drops (4).

Practice your backpedaling. The faster you can go back on a bird, the closer to the net you can play, allowing you to take advantage of weak shots. Imagine you are Willie Mays going back on a deep fly ball to center field, or Steve Young setting up to throw a pass. Finish a jog by running backward, which uses alternate muscles otherwise neglected. Look back over first one shoulder then the other to avoid smashing into things.

DOUBLES STRATEGY

The basic shots in doubles are the same as in singles: drive, smash, clear, and drop. And the goals of both games remain the same: maneuvering the opponent into a vulnerable position for a smash. Both games demand deception in stroking, and both singles and doubles players must mix their strokes and conceal their intent by using the same stance and swing on every shot.

But doubles is more of an attacking game than singles. And the short serve that drops close to the net is standard in doubles. Teamwork, not an issue in singles, is vital in doubles play. Because there is less court to cover, stamina is not as critical in doubles. Wily, experienced teammates commonly whip athletic rookies.

Beginners will find doubles strategy more daunting than singles strategy. Both players on a doubles team must know their responsibilities and be aware of where their partner is at all times. Such a coordinated effort is a product of hours of play together.

Some basic strategy should be plotted out in a pregame conference. Ask questions of each other. Who will take the net after service? Who covers smashes at the centerline? Who covers the forecourt after a partner's smash?

The main goal in doubles is to attack by hitting the shuttle downward as sharply as possible into an undefended area. The team that prevails is frequently the one that first puts the opponents on the defensive—that is, forces them to hit the shuttle up.

Smashing toward the center of the court can create confusion over which partner should make the return. (To the attacker's delight, often neither or both respond.) This center shot also reduces the possible return angles, making it easier to anticipate its placement.

Offensive Formations

Before a doubles team starts play, the partners must decide which of four basic formations they will use. The systems are quite flexible, and players will often slide from one to another in the heat of a rally.

Side-by-Side. In the side-by-side system (Fig. 20), the areas of responsibility are divided along the centerline. This system should not be used unless both partners have about the same ability and experience, and even then it's often discarded for one of the other formations.

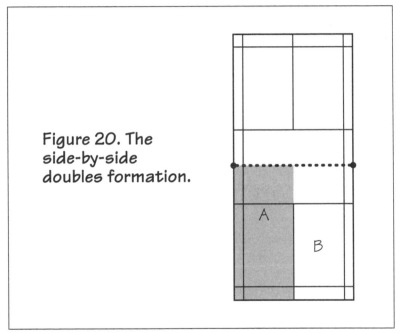

Figure 20. The side-by-side doubles formation.

Even if a team does commit to the side-by-side, there are times in midrally when it will be temporarily abandoned. For example, your partner may rush a drop and you instinctively fill the backcourt. Calling out "Mine!" and "Yours!" to your partner can ease such switches.

The side-by-side formation has several drawbacks, most notably the way it stifles a team's attack. Players in the left court are not able to use their forehand as effectively as in other formations, players in the right court must rely too heavily on their backhand, and confusion often reigns in the center. (Usually, left-court players should cover center smashes with the stronger forehand.)

The side-by-side system can also break down if the opposition effectively pressures one player. Repeated shots to one side can wear out one player while the other watches helplessly.

Front-and-Back. The front-and-back system (Fig. 21) is a favorite of mixed doubles teams. The front player—usually the woman—is responsible for the area between the short service line and the net; the back player covers the area from the short service line to the end line.

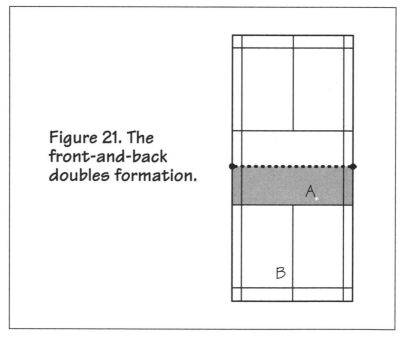

Figure 21. The front-and-back doubles formation.

The front player sets up close to the net—but not so close that her arm movement is restricted—and somewhat left of center to favor her forehand. During play, she slides back and forth laterally in the forecourt, hitting only those shuttles she is confident she can handle cleanly. She tries to hit shots that force the opposition to hit *up*. This is easier said than done, for quite frequently there is time enough only for a quick stab or a flick of the wrist.

The backcourt player is forever forcing the attack, smashing every chance he gets. Only as a last resort does he hit a clear or a drop.

One advantage of the front-and-back system is that one player is always at the net to put away weak returns. An effective one-two punch, for both beginners and masters, is for the back-court player to hit an effective smash or drop and for the fore-court player to move forward to cut off a weak return. As with top tennis players who serve strong and charge the net, this puts a lot of pressure on opponents.

The weakness of the front-and-back system lies in the mid-court near the sidelines. The shot hit just over the net player and in front of the back player can cause each to hesitate, and that's usually enough to put them on the defensive.

Diagonal. In the seldom-used diagonal formation (Fig. 22), the player in the left court covers the left triangle, including the end line, and the player on the right has the rest of the court, including the net.

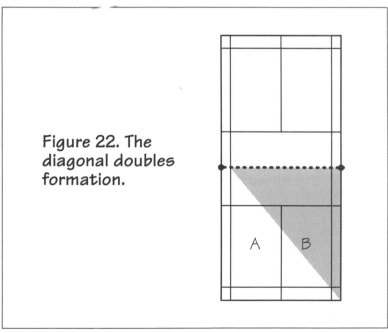

Figure 22. The diagonal doubles formation.

This system is hampered by the absence of visible boundary lines separating the players' domains. It is especially difficult for a diagonal team to handle shots hit to the deep corners.

Rotation (Combination). In the rotation, or combination, system (Fig. 23), teammates rotate counterclockwise, alternating between front-and-back and side-by-side, depending on whether the team is defending or attacking. It is widely used in both men's and women's doubles because it borrows the best offensive and defensive qualities of other formations.

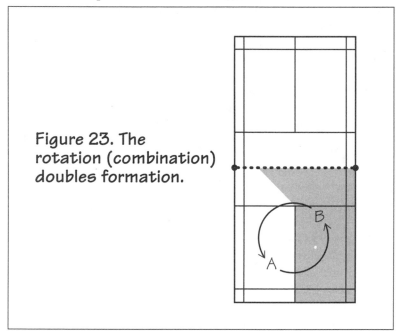

Figure 23. The rotation (combination) doubles formation.

Play begins with players in a side-by-side formation. If the shuttle is hit to the right forecourt, the player on the right moves to the net, while the player on the left shifts to the backcourt. The net player slides left to favor her stronger forehand, knowing that she must cover some of the court behind her as well. Her partner adjusts by moving toward the right forecourt.

If you have just hit defensively—that is, up—switch to the side-by-side formation. The front-and-back is an inadequate defense against an attack, because the net player has no time to react and her partner simply can't defend the entire backcourt against a smash. On the other hand, when attacking, the front-and-back formation is superior.

Players using the rotation system must guard against the temptation to move clockwise. Alert opponents will try to force the left-court player forward and the right-court player back.

When executed properly, however, the rotation system overcomes most disadvantages of other alignments.

MIXED DOUBLES STRATEGY

Mixed doubles—men and women playing as teammates—involves all the skill and excitement of singles. Because badminton doesn't require brute strength, it is the ideal game for men and women to share. This gender balance has helped make badminton the number one participant sport in Great Britain, surpassing such traditional favorites as soccer, cricket, and rugby.

The front-and-back system is the formation of choice in mixed doubles. Typically, the woman plays the forecourt and tries to control the net, while the man roams the backcourt. This is reversed if the woman is the more powerful player.

The forecourt player's goal is to control the attack by keeping the shuttle directed downward with half-court and net shots. She should put away any loose (high and short) shots around the net. Clears, deep drives, and smashes should be left for her partner.

The man's goal is to play the returns from the backcourt with quick, deceptive strokes aimed at forcing weak returns that can then be smashed by him or his partner.

The opposition tries to force both players out of position. Serves to the man tend to be low and short; to the woman, high and deep, where her strengths may be neutralized. Once the woman has left the net, opponents should try to keep her away until a smash can win the rally.

In competitive mixed doubles, players should attack at every opportunity. After the man's shot, the woman should move to the net, racket held high, ready to smash a weak return. Neither player should hit defensively unless forced to.

Attacking does not always mean smashing. A forecourt player with an effective drop can force an opponent to hit up.

Teamwork is vital. Rather than trying to score with every shot, partners should strive to produce a weak return that can then be exploited. This is the basic offensive tactic in mixed doubles.

Other tactics include hitting smashes at the woman, who is closer and has less time to react, and keeping the man running with smashes, drives, and drops. Avoid hitting high to the deeper player. Try not to let either opponent get set for a good shot.

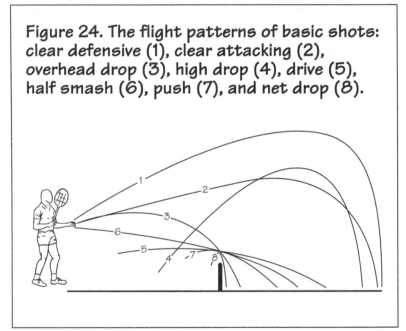

Figure 24. The flight patterns of basic shots: clear defensive (1), clear attacking (2), overhead drop (3), high drop (4), drive (5), half smash (6), push (7), and net drop (8).

The half-court shot, highly effective in mixed doubles, is a drive that barely clears the net and lands in the opponent's court 6 to 12 feet from the net. This shot is generally hit straight ahead if the opponents have good position and cross-court if they are out of position. Ideally, this shot passes the forecourt player and then quickly drops to the floor, forcing the backcourt player to move forward and to the side, retrieving it off his shoe tops or not at all. A well-placed half-court shot is difficult to attack, leaving the opponents only straight-ahead half-court drives and net drops.

Another advantage of a well-placed half-court shot is that the woman, thinking she has a play, often starts toward the sideline, thereby causing the man to hesitate. If the woman doesn't quickly realize her mistake and retreat, she may hinder or obstruct her own partner's shot.

A common pitfall is hitting the half-court shot so high or so hard that it reaches the backcourt player above waist level, permitting an offensive return.

A good mixed doubles team will be alert to the necessity of changing positions during play. If, for example, the woman charges a front-corner drop shot, taking her out of position for the return, her partner must move up to help in the opposite forecourt. When the woman returns, the partners may for a time play side-by-side.

Serving

As in singles, the serve in mixed doubles must be stroked below waist level. This puts the serving team on the defensive. To counter this disadvantage, you should employ deception when serving. Whether you intend to send the bird high or low, deep or shallow, left or right, try to use the same stance and arm swing. The goal of this deception is to retard your opponent's reaction time, however slightly.

The woman usually serves from near the centerline and just behind the front service line (Fig. 25). From there, she can easily move to the forecourt after the serve. The man usually takes a deeper serving position to facilitate his move to the backcourt. He generally serves from about 6 feet behind the short service line. If so, his partner should stand near the T, the intersection of the centerline and short service line, so as not to block the view of the returning opponent.

When a right-handed male is serving from the odd court, his partner usually takes a position to the left of the centerline rather than moving wide to the right.

When the male is returning service, his female partner usually assumes one of the three positions noted in Figure 26, depending on the strengths of the serving team and the strategy of the receiving team.

Position 1 assumes an attacking front-and-back play position and is most effective when the male returner can pressure opponents with his quickness and return skills.

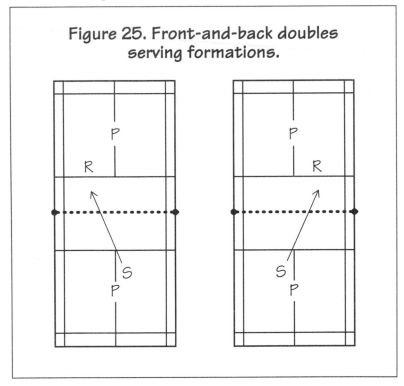

Figure 25. Front-and-back doubles serving formations.

Position 2, with the woman at midcenter court, is used when the service return exerts good pressure but opponents consistently counter with powerful cross-court drives, which are better returned by the female than by the male trying to recover after his service return.

Position 3 is used when the male returner is unable to retreat to the back of the court in time. This could be because of a lack of quickness, poor return skills, or the good, low serves of the opponent.

The obvious disadvantage of positions 2 and 3 is that the female must work her way to the forecourt, whereas in position 1 she starts there.

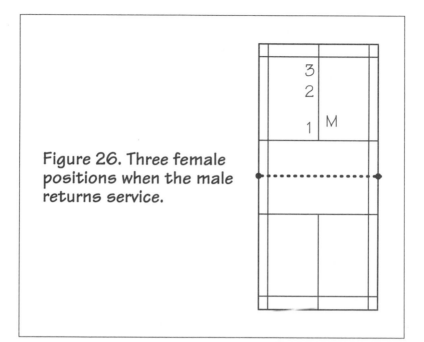

Figure 26. Three female
positions when the male
returns service.

Here are some tips for women in mixed doubles:

- Have a good serve and service return. Because
  they come into play with every rally, they are the
  most important shots in badminton.
- Defense the drops. Many players like to return
  service with net drops, a tactic the woman must
  counter. Some coaches suggest that women in
  mixed doubles matches assume the opponent will
  hit a net drop on each shot.

  If a drop is hit, the woman should attempt to
  catch the shuttle above the net cord and hit a
  smash to win the rally. If she succeeds with some
  regularity, opponents will abandon drop shots in
  favor of half-court shots, and the woman's anticipation should change accordingly.

- Move to the sidelines to cut off half-court shots. Your goal is to anticipate and return weak shots with your own half-court shots that zip just past the outstretched racket of your grunting opponent. Contact the shuttle as high as possible, directing it downward. To improve anticipation, adjust your ready position slightly to the side from which your opponent is hitting. If your opponent moves right, respond by sliding left. If, for example, he is hitting from the deep right sideline, take a position about halfway between that sideline and the centerline. From there, you should be able to turn weak shots into winners, and it will take a great shot to beat you.
- So that you don't have to rely on positions 2 and 3 above, choose a partner with a great service return. (He should also have a cool car and a great personality.)

Here are some tips for men in mixed doubles:

- Choose a partner who is quick enough to return the deep serve and still return to the forecourt for the next shot.
- Attack at every opportunity. Don't hit defensively unless it's unavoidable. Having said that, don't try to score with every shot. Instead, work to produce a weak return that you or your partner can exploit.
- Hit smashes at the woman and drives and drops at the man. Try to keep your opponents running and off-balance.
- Be alert to the need to cover for your partner if she is pulled from position.
- Be tolerant of your partner. As former badminton champion Donald Paup says, "While you can see all of her mistakes, she is likely to see none of yours."

Mixed doubles strategy should incorporate the following:

- Be deceptive, especially when stroking drive and net shots.
- Avoid hitting clears, since the front-and-back position poorly defends the responding smash.
- Use cross-court shots when the opponents are out of position or when the shuttle can be hit from above the waist.
- Disrupt the woman-in-front, man-in-back formation.

BASIC STRATEGY POINTS FOR SINGLES OR DOUBLES

As you strive to improve, keep in mind the following simple points of strategy:

- Return to a good base position after every shot.
- Assume the ready position and be prepared to move in any direction.
- Stray no farther than necessary from your base to hit shots.
- Hit every possible shot overhead, while the shuttle is still above the net.
- Hit *down* on every shuttle that can be struck with an attacking stroke.
- Learn your opponent's weakness—deep backhand, smash right at him, round-the-head shot—and play to it.
- Try to hit shots with the same stance and swing to camouflage your intentions.
- Anticipate your opponent's shots to get a good jump.
- Move the shuttle around the court to keep your opponent running.
- Occasionally, return the shuttle repeatedly to the same spot to throw an opponent off-balance.
- Have a purpose with each shot; avoid hitting aimlessly.
- When uncertain what shot to use, hit a high clear.
- Hit all clears deep.
- Hit shots to the center of the opponent's court to reduce the angle of return.

- Play the shuttle well in front of you; if the shuttle passes over your head, it's hard to hit with any power.
- Keep the shuttle in play; avoid unforced errors.
- In singles, stress the long, high serve; in doubles, stress the low, short serve.
- The time-honored guideline is to serve low to the man and deep to the woman. By serving low to the man, you make it harder for him to take his preferred position in the backcourt; similarly, serving deep to the woman lengthens her run to the net. Still, nothing works every time, so guard against predictability.

WINNING
THE MENTAL GAME

···

You will inevitably master the physical skills of badminton long before the mental ones. When learning a new sport, we tend to concentrate on the muscular activities. That's as it should be. Only after developing some strokes can you begin to play the mental game. First you learn to hit the shots, then you learn to "think" in badminton.

And make no mistake, it is a thinking game. Veteran high school badminton coach Len Hill, who has mentored more than one hundred junior national champions, says he has never had a good player who wasn't smart. "Badminton is a lot like chess," he says. "You have to be thinking at least a couple of moves ahead. The best players I've had would lie in bed at night planning out entire rallies, analyzing all the possibilities. They'd fall asleep doing that."

"**Problem solving** is critical in badminton. Intelligence can overcome tremendous physical abilities on the other side of the net."

—Mike Walker, former national champion

Even as a recreational hacker, mastering the so-called inner game of badminton can give you a competitive advantage. If you mentally fortify yourself with the techniques in this chapter, you can become a better player—without hitting a single bird. Strive for the three Cs: consistency, confidence, and especially concentration.

CONCENTRATION

If you talk to accomplished athletes in any sport, you will hear them speak of the importance of concentration, for concentration is at the heart of success in any endeavor, including badminton.

Most everyone knows that concentration has to do with paying attention. Does that mean consciously willing yourself to focus? Is concentration a shrill voice in your head screaming over and over, "Pay attention!" until you do? Maybe at first.

Former national champion Mike Walker, forty-five, tells two stories that point to the importance of concentration in badminton: "I've been in a lot of strange matches, but none more so than when I was playing Tom Carmichael at the national championships. It was a quarter-final match in a converted airplane hangar at an air force base near Omaha. I hit a high serve up near the rafter, when suddenly a blackbird zoomed out and nailed the shuttle. Tom was sputtering hysterically: 'Did you see that?! Did you see that bird?!'

" 'I didn't see anything, Tom. You just missed the shot.'

"For the next four points, three different blackbirds attacked my serves, finally forcing me to admit that there was a problem.

"Since it was an air force base, a general ordered the birds eliminated. So while we tried to continue the match, marksmen set up in a nearby tower to shoot down the culprits. They were firing thirty feet over our heads into the rafters. It was hysterical— and distracting. We finally had to take a five-minute break while they slaughtered the birds. I eventually won the match, and all those bird-tainted points counted."

Another time the distractions were too great for even Walker to overcome. He was playing for the U.S. national team against Canada. "It was a Thomas Cup match in Quebec City, and we're tied going into my final match," he recalls. "If I win, we go to Indonesia for the finals. I won the first game easily, and in the second game my opponent was clearly tired. I was up by four or five points when the lights went out. It had never happened in two days there, but it happened twice more in that game, both times when I was well ahead. Each time my opponent got a nice ten-minute rest. I lost the second game 15–13. In the third game, I was up 8–1 when it happened again. Then twice more. I eventually lost 18–16. We protested, but it did no good. It showed me that the sport was no longer being played on an amateur basis."

Focus is delicate, elusive. Pay close attention to the trees and you may miss the forest, and vice versa.

Eventually, if you stay with it, you will learn to relax and focus more naturally. Once you master the strokes and know when to use them, you may be able to turn game control over to your now well-developed instincts.

Your conscious mind, however, will want to interfere. Consider this athletic equation:

$$Performance = Potential - Interference$$

Performance is how well you actually do—your results; potential is a measurement of the best performance you are capable of at any given moment; interference is the mental static produced by the conscious mind. When pressure is minimal, the mind may become distracted: "Wonder where Debbie is right now. . . . How about those Knicks? . . . Boy, do I look stunning in these shorts!" As pressure mounts, so do self-doubts and anxiety, two other prime causes of mental static. The conscious mind rushes in, usually to provide a litany of advice: "Tight on the left hand . . . easy with the right . . . deep breaths . . . eye on the bird . . . head down . . . slow backswing . . . follow through . . . whoops!"

With all that advice raining down on you, is it any wonder that you're tighter than last year's pants?

And what happens when you're tight? The unwanted contraction of only a few extra muscle fibers in the arms is enough to turn the racket face off-line by a few degrees, turning a handsome drive into a shallow bloop.

A reduction of mental interference will improve performance, even with no change in potential (read: practice). In other words, get your head screwed on right, and you can become a better player without even picking up a racket.

But the overactive conscious mind does not react well to being told to butt out. (It's rather like ordering yourself to sleep.) Instead, you will have to rely on deceit. Some coaches suggest distracting the conscious mind by focusing on something only marginally related to the task at hand. By giving it something else to chew on, the subconscious is left unfettered. Two ways to distract that pesky conscious mind are by positive association and visualization.

To associate positively, immerse yourself in positive recollections. Suppose you are serving for the match. Like everyone, you've had both good and bad moments in the past. For best results, think about the successes and discard the failures. Replay an imaginary tape that you might call "My Greatest Hits."

First cousin to positive association, visualization is a type of mental rehearsal in which you conjure up detailed visions of the activity before you do it.

The first step in visualization is to relax. Use a method that works for you. You might close your eyes and take a few deep breaths, recite your favorite mantra, or play a mental videotape of a winning moment.

Focus on the finer points of the swing. Immerse yourself in the swing. See it as one fluid whole. Hear the twang of shuttle hitting strings; feel the heft of the racket, your fingers curling around the shaft; see the bird streaking toward its target.

Visualization takes dedicated practice. The up side is that you can practice it anywhere—in a bed or bathtub, at a bus stop—and the rewards can be staggering. I have interviewed and profiled forty world-class athletes, and most attribute some, if not most, of their success to visualization.

Research suggests that muscles respond to visualization of an act almost as if you did the act. Thus, the more intensely you visualize the perfect smash, the more entrenched it will be in your muscle memory. This kind of memory operates almost entirely on the subconscious level, which helps explain how you can play a shot beautifully but can't explain it to others.

The power of visualization received a lot of publicity in the seventies with the revelations of several famous athletes. Golfer Jack Nicklaus said that he never hit a shot without first seeing the ball's perfect flight followed by its "sitting up there high and white and pretty on the green." A successful shot, according to Nicklaus, was 50 percent visualization, 40 percent setup, and only 10 percent swing.

STUDY THE OPPONENT

The time before a match should be spent limbering up—not just physically, but mentally as well. Whether the player on the other side of the net is a stranger or your weekly partner, study his or her play. Besides such obvious matters as whether your opponent is left- or right-handed or walks with a limp, study the subtleties. Routinely ask yourself the following questions:

- What are his weaknesses? Favorite shots?
- How is his net play? Is the forehand or backhand better?
- Does he get height on his clears, or can they be intercepted?
- Can he hit a clear from baseline to baseline with forehand and backhand?
- Does he avoid hitting a backhand?

- How does he handle shots to his body?
- What are his serving tendencies? Does he telegraph it?
- How does he play high and low serves?
- Does he display different mannerisms when he's tired?

The following are tips for winning the mental game, from former world-class badminton player Derek Talbot:

- Always allow for a complete ten-minute warmup before a match.
- Two minutes before a match, do sixty seconds of stomach breathing. At the change of ends in a match, a few seconds of stomach breathing keeps the brain alert, even though you may be tired.
- Given the choice of ends at the start of a match, always choose the worst end first. It is better to finish the match on the best side of the court, and in the first game, before either player has acclimatized, it is less of a disadvantage to have the worst end. The quality of the ends is usually governed by background, lighting, or both.
- Play your normal game in the first instance against an unknown opponent. If it's not successful, then try a style of play that is the opposite of your opponent's.
- If your opponent is on a winning streak, never allow him to rush you. If he tries, take your time in between rallies.
- Drink only plain water or glucose drink during a match, and limit these to only a few mouthfuls.
- Remember that there is no such thing as a perfect player. Your opponent is only human, despite the doubts you may have during slumps. He has weaknesses and can be beaten.

Smart players will make adjustments that help them succeed. For example, if your opponent begins shaking out his arms or displaying other signs of fatigue, pick up the pace and try to move him quickly around the court. If your opponent reveals an early weakness, exploit it. If his backhand is weak, hit a couple of shots deep to his forehand that pull him to the right, then pepper his backhand.

ATTITUDE

The biggest difference between the competent and the excellent in any sport is mental preparation. Successful athletes find a way to remain, or quickly regain, calm. To be effective, you must keep a check on counterproductive emotions. Some play better than others when they're mad; no one plays well in a rage. Analyze missed shots, but don't dwell on them.

PRESSURE

As you improve and face stiffer competition, the pressure mounts. It is pressure that causes a great player to net a smash that she's made thousands of times before.

Picture this scenario: You're behind in a match against a pretty good player in your neighborhood or club. You have to win your serve to stay in the game. There are a few people watching, and you feel the rivalry. Your guts are twisting like a wet rope. Now that's pressure. Most everyone feels it at one time or another. The real question is whether you can control it. Successful people don't dodge pressure; they make it work to their benefit.

On the other hand, others seem to block it out entirely. George Brett, destined for the Baseball Hall of Fame, was once asked about the pressure of playing his sport. His response, as I paraphrase it, is equally applicable to badminton. "Pressure?" Brett said, "Ha, this isn't pressure. This is just a game. Pressure is feeding a family of four on a fixed income."

GETTING BETTER

A misconception stunting the growth of badminton is that the game is somehow dainty or delicate. It is sometimes derided by men as a "girls' game," in part because of its lightweight racket, dancing shuttle, and small court dimensions. If, however, it is played correctly, with skill, it is actually a game that demands exceptional vigor, quickness, and power. In short, it is a sport for the physically fit.

If you become serious about badminton, try to advance your skills both on and off the court. Play lots of games, yes, but also maintain a workout regimen focused on the skills needed to become the best badminton player in the world—or at least on your block.

Seek out opponents and partners who are slightly better than you, who will demonstrate new techniques and skills. Beating up on weaker players may briefly fuel your feelings of superiority, but it won't help your badminton game nearly as much as some hard-fought, well-played, learning-intensive defeats. Against good opponents, you will learn how quickly you must dart around the court, how accurately you must hit your shots, how to think under pressure, and how hard it is to score.

Even if you prefer doubles, play a lot of singles. This will increase your stamina and reveal weaknesses that might go undetected in a doubles game.

Then work on those weaknesses. For example, instead of running around backhands and turning them into forehands, hang tough and hit backhand after backhand, working on proper technique. Ask your practice opponent to hit to your backhand. Don't assume that you've perfected a shot just because you hit five good ones in a row. Set higher standards for yourself. Can you hit it well thirty times in a row? Practice until you can.

It is the willingness to practice that separates masters from the middling, no matter what the pursuit. As sports philosopher George Leonard says, "The master of any game is generally a master of practice."

The master's journey begins as soon as you commit to learning a new skill, whether it's how to knit, cook, weld, or play dominoes. But sports provide an especially effective launching pad for the pursuit of excellence, because the results of training are clearly visible. In most sports, you can plot your progress, either with statistics or by comparing yourself with other players.

The master's journey is not an inexorably upward slope. Instead, it consists of brief spurts of progress, each followed by a slight decline to a plateau usually somewhat higher than the plateau that preceded it. It looks like this:

Clearly, then, you have to be prepared—and content—to spend a lot of time on plateaus; you have to push yourself to practice even when no progress is evident. Only with diligent practice will you ingrain the shots in muscle memory, the behavioral autopilot that works on the subconscious level.

According to George Leonard, author of *Mastery*, there are five keys to opening the doors to mastery:

1. **Instruction: Be open to first-rate teaching.**
2. **Practice: Think of the word as a noun, not just a verb, as something you are, not just something you do.**
3. **Surrender: Give in to your teacher and the demands of your discipline.**
4. **Intentionality: Muster all the mental energy and vision you can behind the pursuit.**
5. **The Edge: Push yourself beyond your ordinary limits.**

Even if you're bursting with talent, practice is essential; in fact, you may have to practice harder, because we tend to ease up when skills come easily. We're tempted, in George Leonard's words, "not to penetrate to the marrow of a practice." Instead of being frustrated with plateaus, learn to revel in them. If you can enjoy them as much as the upslopes, you are on the path to mastery.

Chris Jogis, former U.S. singles champion, used to train five hours a day. "Badminton is an easy sport to play in the backyard," he says, "but as a serious sport, it's definitely not easy. It takes a lot of training to be good and a lot of experience to compete at the top level. We want people to know we're serious athletes."

ON-COURT PRACTICE

High-quality on-court practice sessions often depend on someone who can accurately and consistently feed birds to the hitters, either by hand or racket. When hand feeding, the feeder can have several birds nested on her arm. She can toss them underhand or, holding them by the base, throw them like darts. If the feeder has good racket control, she can hit underhand strokes to a specific spot on the court.

Don't be in too big of a hurry to start hitting shuttles, however. Footwork drills combined with shadow swinging make for an effective pregame warmup. Start from the ready position—facing the net, racket in front of your body, feet about shoulder width apart, weight on the balls of your feet, knees slightly bent. From there, imagine consecutive returns going to all four corners and both sidelines, then move accordingly, trying to return to the ready position each time. For example, imagine that your invisible opponent hits a deep clear to the right corner and quickly retreat to the spot from which you can best handle that shot. Next imagine a deep clear to the left corner and move accordingly. Repeat for a variety of drops. Work on anticipation, quickness, and footwork.

On-Court Drills

To develop racket awareness, you can practice running while carrying a bird on your racket. Run to an established turnaround point and back without dropping the bird. If you do drop it, pick it up, put it back on the racket, and continue. Use a proper grip at all times, either forehand—palm up—or backhand—palm down.

Once you've mastered that, try bouncing the bird on your racket as you run. This will develop eye-hand coordination and emphasize proper grip.

Hold the bird well in front of the body, drop it, and tap it in the air. Alternate between forehand and backhand taps. At first you will hit the bird high in the air, but practice will reduce the height to 1 to 2 feet. With enough players, you can turn this into a relay race. Each player should bounce the bird at least three times en route.

If you have a partner who is as committed to improvement as you are, try the following workout. The first five drills will take about half an hour. If you have a full hour, go on to the next five drills; otherwise, save them for another day. It's helpful to have plenty of shuttles for these drills.

1. 5 minutes: Bat the bird back and forth to loosen up.
2. 6 minutes: Move forward and hit soft underhand net shots to each other. They can go straight over the net or at an angle, but they should be aimed to barely clear the net and fall quickly to the other side. This drill develops touch and improves wrist and finger control.
3. 6 minutes: One player smashes and the other replies with clears. Switch roles after 3 minutes. (Smashes can be exhausting.)
4. 6 minutes: One player hits to the backhand of the opponent, who responds with a backhand overhead drop. Switch after 3 minutes.
5. 6 minutes: One player hits clears to the forehand corner, and the opponent replies by hitting forehand overhead drops. Switch roles after 3 minutes.
6. 6 minutes: One player hits high serves to the other's forehand and backhand, which are returned by smashes. Switch after 3 minutes.

7. 8 minutes: One player hits low serves to the left and right sides of both courts. The receiver rushes the net, tries to meet the shuttle early, and hits it sharply down. Switch after 4 minutes.
8. 6 minutes: One player smashes, and the other returns with underhand drops. Switch after 3 minutes.
9. 4 minutes: Both players stand at their midcourts and exchange low, hard drives aimed down the lines, crosscourt, or right at each other.
10. 6 minutes: Players alternate hitting clears and drops—a basic singles tactic—trying to keep the shuttle in play as long as possible.

These routines are merely guidelines designed to offer variety and balance. If you have a particular weakness, you will want to spend more time on that than on your strengths.

The following shots are those that trouble most beginners:

- Low serve—hitting too high.
- High serve—hitting too shallow.
- Clear—hitting too shallow.
- Smash—hitting too deep.

OFF-COURT PRACTICE

Shadow Swinging

Teachers often have their students practice the swinging motion before they even see a shuttle. In this way, new players can concentrate on the variables of the swing instead of obsessing on the bird. Ideally, you picture the entire stroke, break it down into components, then put it back together again. Thus you develop a sense of both the overall stroke and the individual parts.

A badminton racket has little potential force because of its light weight, but you can compensate for this with a supple wrist snap at the moment of impact. This snap speeds the racket through the air, increasing the force of the stroke. To accomplish this, wrist flexibility and strength of the small wrist flexor muscles are essential. Despite the emphasis on wristing the shuttle, beginners should keep in mind that overheads and smashes also demand a full arm.

Wall Practice

To play badminton well, you need to hit a lot of birds. But what if you don't have a partner of like ability? Walls can be used for practicing almost every stroke. Diligent wall practice will acquaint players with the universal grip; reinforce rhythm, footwork, stance, and body alignment; and strengthen the arm and wrist muscles used in badminton.

Concrete and brick walls provide more bounce than wooden walls, but most walls will work for at least some shots. An 8-foot wall cannot be used to practice lobs and clears but will do fine for drops, drives, and net shots. According to badminton coach Cheah Swee Ming, wall practice is especially valuable for teaching the backhand overhead clear. The physical demands of wall practice can be adjusted to every level of proficiency. Two walls at right angles offer even more variety.

When former badminton champion Mike Walker offers tips for rookies, he begins with the old bromide: Watch the bird. "People tend to focus on where the opponent is hitting from rather than the flight of the shuttle," he says. "A good way to get used to watching the bird is to hit against a wall. The wall will return it every time, and always at a different angle. You can't beat the wall."

Here are some recommendations for successful wall practice:

- For group practice, each player will need at least 6 feet, measured along the base of the wall, to avoid getting in someone else's way. Figure on about 9 feet between the players and the wall, depending on the strength of their hits. The wall should be at least 20 feet high to accommodate lobs and clears. It's useful to have a line 5 feet off the ground to indicate the height of the net.
- Emphasize wrist movement. Frequent wall practice strengthens wrists and improves reflexes. Because the

shuttle rebounds so fast from a wall, the wrist will naturally come into play. The beginner won't have time to switch grips between forehand and backhand and so should use what in tennis is known as the continental, or bread-slicing, grip.

- Work for stroke consistency. Hit each stroke with control. Have a purpose with each shot, and honestly evaluate your results.
- Strive for a rhythm. This will help you keep the shuttle in play and minimize frustration.
- Work on forehand and backhand strokes simultaneously. Beginners lack the shuttle control necessary to focus exclusively on one or the other.
- Work on the proper serve, including correct stance. Standing about 4 $1/2$ feet from the wall, hit a regular high service stroke, then quickly assume a defensive position, because the wall returns the shuttle quickly.
- As you improve, strive to hit all shots with proper form and footwork, which should be the same for wall practice as for court play.
- To avoid boredom, probably the biggest obstacle to regular practice, invent games. Challenge yourself. Count the number of consecutive shots you can hit. Break your own records.

Wall Drills for Beginners. If you are a beginner, start your wall drills by hitting shots that don't come right back to you. This will be easy in the beginning when you lack control. Practice a variety of shots—forehand and backhand clears, smashes, overhead-underhand drops, and serves. Try to anticipate where the next shot will go, and move quickly to get there in the fewest steps. As with court play, have a purpose with every shot.

Two players with a little experience should be able to practice together against a common wall. Lobs can be traded with one player hitting forehands and the other backhands.

Here are some points to consider when hitting against walls:

- Practice hitting the bird delicately on drop shots.
- Aim for consistency.

- Get the racket back in plenty of time—usually as you move into position for the shot.
- Maintain good balance while trying to reach the bird in the fewest steps possible.
- When serving, work on a smooth wrist snap for high serves; low serves should barely clear the line representing the net.
- Control the intensity of practice by varying the angle of shots; the height of shots; hard and soft shot combinations; and forehand and backhand combinations.
- Wall practice should be balanced with court play, lest you become bored to tears. And walls don't offer you a realistic feel of the flight of your shots. Because you don't see the shuttle's complete trajectory, you don't benefit from "knowledge of results"—that is, whether your shots would have landed in or out.

EXERCISE

If you play an opponent of comparable ability, the fitter player will usually prevail. So if you wish to advance beyond the level of hacker, you must also work out off the court and away from the wall.

Whether you're a badminton player or a chess master, it's important to satisfy your aerobic needs. Sustaining an elevated heartbeat at least fifteen minutes a day three or more times a week will hone cardiovascular endurance and defend against heart disease. According to Dr. Kenneth Cooper, the godfather of aerobics, prolonged, low-intensity exercise improves physical endurance better than brief, explosive workouts. You can most easily achieve this through regular aerobic exercise that includes one or more of the following: running, brisk walking, cycling, swimming, rowing, rope skipping, cross-country skiing, or aerobic dance.

More and more, top-flight badminton players lift weights. Strengthening specific parts of your body will increase your badminton potential. Back, stomach, forearms, and wrists are particularly important.

Overhead shots require a lot of bending backward, and forecourt shots require a forward bend, both of which stress the back. Strengthening stomach muscles is important for back protection. We now know that full elbow-to-knee situps are hard on the back, so instead, raise the torso off the ground only a few inches, tightening the stomach muscles. Do ten of these crunches a few times a day.

Here are some basic tips for avoiding injury and increasing the enjoyment of exercise:

- Don't overdo it.
- Realize that "No pain, no gain" is a myth.
- Use adequate footwear.
- Watch your form and posture.
- Don't bounce when stretching.
- Avoid high-impact aerobics.
- Warm up and cool down.

Despite their good intentions, half the people who take up a new exercise program quit within six months. Here are some ways to boost your stick-to-it-iveness:

- Seek convenience.
- Start slow and easy.
- Set realistic exercise goals.
- Find a support group.
- Add variety.
- Record your progress.

The following are the stories of three badminton players who pursued excellence.

Meiling Okuno, at 5-foot-3 and 110 pounds, is proof that you don't have to be big to sting a badminton bird. One of the top five American women, she has twice been U.S. singles runner-up.

"Like most people, I started playing in the backyard," she says. "I loved the running around. Then, before my freshman year of high school, I took a badminton class at summer school. With that push, I played all four years of high school, winning the Central Coast Section [consisting of about ninety high schools] the last three years.

"At age eighteen, I was at the top of a very small pyramid. Then I started playing adults and discovered reality. In the first round of my first tournament, I played the national champion, Cheryl Carton, and lost 11–0, 11–1.

"I stayed with it, though, mainly because I had a close circle of friends who liked to play. After I married Russ, we started going to tournaments together. A turning point was one in San Diego, which all the top players entered. After I beat two of them, I thought, 'Hmmm, maybe there's something to this.' Russ urged me to go for it, and so I did.

"Badminton has allowed me to travel to places—Britain, Japan, Indonesia, China—I never would have seen otherwise. At the 1987 World Championships in Beijing, China, I played in front of about thirty thousand screaming fans. It was like a hockey game.

"Now I'm trying to make the Olympic team. But even if I don't, even if I stop playing at a top competitive level, I'll continue to bat birds around. There's just a great group of people who play this game."

Mike Walker has been playing badminton for thirty-five years, and in that time he has won more than thirty national titles in the junior, open, and senior divisions.

"I was eleven when I first walked into a gym where badminton was played," he says. "The recreation director there, a man named Ned, was a badminton-crazy man. He stuck a racket in anyone's hand who could walk and chew gum. He probably turned on over four hundred kids to the sport just in that one gym.

"I can still remember the joy I felt when I learned that I could actually hit the bird over the net. I got into a junior program and played once a week for six weeks before entering a tournament.

When I won the eleven-and-under boys' singles, I was hooked. I still have the trophy—it's about three inches high.

"I didn't win another tournament for a year and a half. But I kept playing, at least a couple of times a week for the rest of my life. Ned got me to teach badminton skills to other kids. I learned early on to give back to the sport. That needs to happen all over the country, because it's what makes badminton grow.

"I won my first national title at seventeen—the eighteen-and-under boys' doubles—and the next year I swept, winning the singles, doubles, and mixed doubles. My first adult open title was at age twenty-four.

"The best thing about badminton is that it's a constant challenge, always different. I plan to play until I'm a hundred—at least."

Russ Okuno is a "B" player in California, but because of the number of badminton players in California, he would be an "A" player in many other parts of the country.

"I started playing badminton quite late, at about nineteen. I was a competitive swimmer, but our coach liked to expose us to lots of different activities. He took us backpacking, skiing; then one day we saw some badminton rackets sticking out of his bag. We were too ignorant to know what they were. We asked him what he was going to do with the tennis rackets.

"He invited us to go with him and play. I loved badminton, and after I quit competitive swimming, I kept playing. In college I took P.E. classes in badminton. I found out it was an intercollegiate sport. My school didn't have a team, so I formed a badminton club, and we competed against other schools. Badminton became a great way for me to channel energies, have fun, get better, meet new people, and travel a little.

"My wife is on the national team, and for the last ten years I've essentially managed her career. That's put me in touch with some good coaching. I still feel I'm getting better. I believe that forty-one-year-old Russ would beat thirty-year-old Russ. On the other hand, since 1985 I've played hundreds of matches against my wife, and I haven't taken one game from her."

LAWS OF BADMINTON

···

As amended and adopted by the IBF
through May 1992

1. Court

1.1   The court shall be a rectangle with measurements laid
      out as in Fig. 2b (exception: Law 1.5), defined by lines
      1 $^1/_2$" wide.

1.2   The lines, preferably white or yellow, shall be easily dis-
      tinguishable.

1.3.1 To show the zone in which a shuttle of correct pace
       lands when tested (Law 4.4), an additional four marks
       1 $^1/_2$" by 1 $^1/_2$" may be made inside each singles sideline
       of the right service court, 1'9" to 3'3" from the back
       boundary line.

1.3.2 In making these marks, their width shall be within the
       measurement given, i.e., the marks will be from 1'9" to
       1'10 $^1/_2$" and from 3'1 $^1/_2$" to 3'3" from the outside of the
       back boundary line.

1.4   All lines form part of the area that they define.

1.5   Where space does not permit the marking out of a court
      for doubles, a court may be marked out for singles only,
      as in Fig. 2a. The back boundary lines become also the
      long service lines, and the posts, or the strips of mater-
      ial representing them (Law 2.2), shall be placed on the
      sidelines.

2. Posts

2.1   The posts shall be 5'1" in height from the surface of the
      court. They shall be sufficiently firm to remain vertical

and keep the net strained as provided in Law 3, and shall be placed on the doubles sideline as shown in Fig. 2b.

2.2 When it is not practical to have posts on the sideline, some method must be used to indicate the position of the sidelines where they pass under the net, e.g., by the use of thin posts or strips of material 1 $\frac{1}{2}$" wide, fixed to the sidelines and rising vertically to the net cord.

2.3 On a court marked for doubles, the posts or strips of material representing the posts shall be placed on the doubles sidelines, regardless of whether singles or doubles is being played.

3. Net

3.1 The net shall be made of fine cord of dark color and even thickness with a mesh not less than 15 mm ($\frac{5}{8}$") and not more than 20 mm ($\frac{3}{4}$").

3.2 The net, from the top of the tape to the bottom of the mesh, shall be 2'6" in height.

3.3 The top of the net shall be edged with a 3" white tape doubled over a cord or cable running through the tape. The tape must rest upon the cord or cable.

3.4 The cord or cable shall be of sufficient size and weight to be firmly stretched flush with the top of the posts.

3.5 The top of the net from the surface of the court shall be 5' at the center of the court and 5'1" over the doubles sidelines.

3.6 There shall be no gaps between the ends of the net and the posts. If necessary, the full depth of the net should be tied at the ends.

4. Shuttle

Principles: The shuttle may be made from natural and/or synthetic materials. Whatever material the shuttle is made from, the flight characteristics should generally be similar to those produced by a natural feathered shuttle with a cork base covered by a thin layer of leather. Having regard to the principles:

4.1 General Design

4.1.1 The shuttle shall have sixteen feathers fixed in the base.

4.1.2 The feathers can have a variable length from 2 $\frac{1}{2}$" to 2 $\frac{3}{4}$", but in each shuttle they shall be the same length when measured from the tip to the top of the base.

4.1.3 The tips of the feathers shall form a circle with a diameter from 2 $\frac{1}{4}$" to 2 $\frac{5}{8}$"

4.1.4 The feathers shall be fastened firmly with thread or other suitable material.

4.1.5 The base shall be:
- 1" to 1 $\frac{1}{8}$" in diameter
- rounded on the bottom

4.2 Weight

The shuttle shall weigh from 4.74 to 5.50 grams.

4.3 Nonfeathered Shuttle

4.3.1 The skirt, or simulation of feathers in synthetic material, replaces natural feathers.

4.3.2 The base is described in Law 4.1.5

4.3.3 Measurements and weight shall be as in Laws 4.1.2, 4.1.3, and 4.2. However, because of the difference in specific gravity and behavior of synthetic material compared with feathers, a variation of up to 10 percent is acceptable.

4.4 Shuttle Testing

4.4.1 To test a shuttle, use a full underhand stroke that makes contact with the shuttle over the back boundary line. The shuttle shall be hit at an upward angle and parallel to the sidelines.

4.4.2 A shuttle of correct pace will land not less than 1'9" and not more than 3'3" short of the other back boundary line.

4.5 Modifications

If there is no variation in the pace, flight, and general design of the shuttle, modifications in the above specifications may be made with the approval of the national organization concerned:

4.5.1　In places where atmospheric conditions due to either altitude or climate make the standard shuttle unsuitable; or

4.5.2　If special circumstances exist that make it otherwise necessary in the interests of the game.

5. Racket

5.1　The hitting surface of the racket shall consist of a pattern of crossed strings connected to a frame and either alternately interlaced or bonded where they cross. The stringing pattern shall be generally uniform and, in particular, not less dense in the center than in any other area.

5.2　The frame of the racket, including the handle, shall not exceed 2'2 $^3/_4$" in overall length and 9" in overall width.

5.3　The overall length of the head shall not exceed 11 $^3/_8$".

5.4　The strung surface shall not exceed 11" in overall length and 8 $^5/_8$" in overall width.

5.5　The racket:

5.5.1　Shall be free of attached objects and protrusions, other than those utilized solely and specifically to limit wear and tear, or vibration, or to distribute weight, or to secure the handle by cord to the player's hand, and which are reasonable in size and placement for such purposes;

5.5.2　Shall be free of any device that makes it possible for a player to change materially the shape of the racket.

6. Approved Equipment

The International Badminton Federation shall rule on any question of whether a racket, shuttle, or other equipment or prototype used in badminton complies with the specifications or is otherwise approved or not approved for play. Such ruling may be undertaken on the Federation's initiative or upon application by any party with a bona fide interest therein, including any player, equipment manufacturer, or national organization.

7. Players

7.1 "Player" applies to all those taking part in a match.
7.2 The singles game shall be played by one player a side; the doubles game by two players a side.
7.3 The side having the right to serve shall be called the serving side, and the opposing side shall be called the receiving side.

8. Toss

8.1 Before commencing play, the two sides shall toss a coin, and the side winning the toss shall exercise the choice in Law 8.1.1 or 8.1.2.
8.1.1 To serve or receive first
8.1.2 To start play at one end of the court or the other.
8.2 The side losing the toss shall then exercise the remaining choice.

9. Scoring

9.1 The opposing sides shall play the best of three games unless otherwise arranged.
9.2 Only the serving side can add a point to its score.
9.3 In doubles and men's singles, a game is won by the first side to score 15 points, except under Law 9.6.
9.4 In women's singles, a game is won by the first side to score 11 points, except as provided in Law 9.6.
9.5.1 If the score becomes 13–13 or 14–14 (9–9 or 10–10 in women's singles), the side that first scored 13 or 14 (9 or 10) shall have the choice of "setting" or "not setting" the game (see Law 9.6).
9.5.2 The choice can only be made when the score is first

reached and must be made before the next service is delivered.

9.5.3   The relevant side (Law 9.5.1) is given the opportunity to set at 14–all (10–all in women's singles) despite any previous decision (by either side) not to set at 13–all (9–all in women's singles).

9.6   If the game has been set, the score is called "Love all," and the side first scoring the set number of points (Law 9.6.1 to 9.6.4) wins the game.

9.6.1   13–all sets to 5 points

9.6.2   14–all sets to 3 points

9.6.3   9–all sets to 3 points

9.6.4   10–all sets to 2 points

9.7   The side winning a game serves first in the next game.

10. Change of Ends

10.1   Players shall change ends:

10.1.1   At the end of the first game;

10.1.2   Prior to the beginning of the third game (if any); and

10.1.3   In the third game, or in a one-game match, when the leading score reaches:
   6 in a game of 11 points
   8 in a game of 15 points
   11 in a game of 21 points

10.2   When players omit to change ends as indicated by Law 10.1, they shall do so as soon as the mistake is discovered, and the existing score shall stand.

11. Service

11.1   In a correct service:

11.1.1   Neither side shall cause undue delay to the delivery of the service;

11.1.2   The server and receiver shall stand within diagonally opposite service courts without touching the boundary lines of these service courts. Some part of both feet of the server and receiver must remain in contact with the surface of the court in a stationary position until the service is delivered (see Law 11.4).

11.1.3 The server's racket shall initially hit the base of the shuttle while the whole of the shuttle is below the server's waist.

11.1.4 The shaft of the server's racket at the instant of hitting the shuttle shall be pointing in a downward direction to such an extent that the whole head of the racket is discernible below the whole server's hand holding the racket;

11.1.5 The movement of the server's racket must continue forward after the start of the service (see Law 11.2) until the service is delivered; and

11.1.6 The flight of the shuttle shall be upward from the server's racket and over the net, so that, if not intercepted, it falls in the receiver's service court.

11.2 Once the players have taken their positions, the first forward movement of the server's racket is the start of the service.

11.3 The server shall not serve before the receiver is ready, but the receiver shall be considered to have been ready if a return of service is attempted.

11.4 The service is delivered when, once started (Law 11.2), the shuttle is hit by the server's racket or the shuttle lands on the floor.

11.5 In doubles, partners may take up any positions that don't block the views of the opposing server or receiver.

12. Singles

12.1 The players shall serve from, and receive in, their respective right service courts when the server has not scored or has scored an even number of points in that game.

12.2 The players shall serve from, and receive in, their respective left service courts when the server has scored an odd number of points in that game.

12.3   If a game is set, the total points scored by the server in that game shall be used to apply Laws 12.1 and 12.2.

12.4   The shuttle is hit alternately by the server and the receiver until a "fault" is made or the shuttle ceases to be in play.

12.5.1   If the receiver makes a fault or the shuttle ceases to be in play because it touches the surface of the court inside the receiver's court, the server scores a point. The server then serves again from the alternate service court.

12.5.2   If the server makes a fault or the shuttle ceases to be in play because it touches the surface of the court inside the server's court, the server loses the right to continue serving, and the receiver then becomes the server, with no point scored by either player.

13. Doubles

13.1   At the start of the game, and each time a side gains the right to serve, the service shall be delivered from the right service court.

13.2   Only the receiver shall return the service. Should the shuttle touch or be hit by the receiver's partner, the serving side scores a point.

13.3.1   After the service is returned, the shuttle can be hit by either player of the serving side and then by either player of the receiving side, and so on, until the shuttle ceases to be in play.

13.3.2   After the service is returned, a player may hit the shuttle from any position on that player's side of the net.

13.4.1   If the receiving side makes a fault or the shuttle ceases to be in play because it touches the surface of the receiving side's court, the serving side scores a point, and the server serves again.

13.4.2   If the serving side makes a fault or the shuttle ceases to be in play because it touches the surface of the serving side's court, the server loses the right to continue serving, with no point scored by either side.

13.5.1 The player who serves at the start of any game shall serve from, or receive in, the right service court when that player's side has not scored or has scored an even number of points, and the left service court otherwise.

13.5.2 The player who receives at the start of any game shall receive in, and serve from, the right service court when that player's side has not scored or has scored an even number of points, and the left service court otherwise.

13.5.3 The reverse pattern applies to partners.

13.5.4 If a game is set, the total points scored by a side in that game shall be used to apply laws 13.5.1 to 13.5.3.

13.6 Until the server's turn ends, service shall be delivered from alternate service courts, except as provided in Laws 14 and 16.

13.7 The right to serve passes consecutively from the initial server to the initial receiver to the initial receiver's partner, and then to either one of the opponents, and then to the opponent's partner, and so on.

13.8 No player shall serve out of turn, receive out of turn, or receive two consecutive services in the same game, except as provided in Laws 14 and 16.

13.9 Either player of the winning side may serve first in the next game, and either player of the losing side may receive.

14. Service Court Errors

14.1 A service court error has been made when a player:

14.1.1 Has served out of turn;

14.1.2 Has served from the wrong service court; or

14.1.3 Has stood in the wrong service court prepared to receive serve, and the serve was delivered.

14.2 When a service court error has been made, then:

14.2.1 If the error is discovered before the next service is delivered, it is a *let* unless only one side was at fault and lost the rally, in which case the error shall not be corrected.

14.2.2 If the error is not discovered before the next service is delivered, it shall not be corrected.

14.3   If there is a *let* because of a service court error, the rally is replayed with the error corrected.

14.4   If a service court error is not to be corrected, play shall proceed without changing the player's new service courts or new order of serving.

15. Faults

It is a fault:

15.1   If a service is not correct (Law 11.1);

15.2   If the server, attempting to serve, misses the shuttle;

15.3   If after passing over the net on service, the shuttle is caught in or on the net;

15.4   If in play, the shuttle:

15.4.1   Lands outside the boundaries of the court;

15.4.2   Passes through or under the net;

15.4.3   Fails to pass the net;

15.4.4   Touches the roof, ceiling, or side walls;

15.4.5   Touches the person or dress of a player; or

15.4.6   Touches any other object or person outside the immediate surroundings of the court. (Local badminton authorities may make their own rules regarding shuttles touching obstructions.)

15.5   If:

15.6   If, when the shuttle is in play, a player:

15.6.1   Touches the net or its supports with racket, person, or dress;

15.6.2   Invades an opponent's court with racket or person in any degree, except as permitted in Law 15.5; or

15.6.3   Prevents an opponent from making a legal stroke where the shuttle is followed over the net;

15.7   Deliberately distracts an opponent by any action, such as shouting or making gestures.

15.8   If, in play, the shuttle:

15.8.1   Is caught and held on the racket and slung during the execution of a stroke;

15.8.2   Is hit twice in succession by the same player with two strokes. A double hit by one player with one stroke is not a fault;

15.8.3 Is hit by a player and the player's partner successively; or

15.8.4 Touches a player's racket and continues toward the back of that player's court.

15.9 If a player is guilty of flagrant, repeated, or persistent offenses under Law 18.

16. Lets

"Let" is called by the umpire, or by a player if there is no umpire, to halt play.

16.1 A let may be given for any unforeseen or accidental occurrence.

16.2 If a shuttle, after passing over the net, is caught in or on the net, it is a let except during service.

16.3 If during service, the server and receiver are both faulted at the same time, it shall be a let.

16.4 If the server serves before the receiver is ready, it shall be a let.

16.5 If the shuttle disintegrates during play or the base separates from the rest of the shuttle, it shall be a let.

16.6 If a line judge is unsighted and the umpire is unable to make a decision, it shall be a let.

16.7 When a let occurs, the play since the last service shall not count, and the player who served shall serve again, except when Law 14 is applicable.

17. Shuttle Not in Play

A shuttle is not in play when:

17.1 It strikes the net and remains attached there or suspended on top;

17.2 It strikes the net or post and starts to fall toward the surface of the court on the striker's side of the net;

17.3   It hits the surface of the court; or

17.4   A fault or let has occurred.

18. Continuous Play, Misconduct, Penalties

18.1   Play shall be continuous from the first service until the match is concluded, except as allowed in Laws 18.2 and 18.3.

18.2   An interval not exceeding five minutes is allowed between the second and third games of all matches in the following situations:

18.2.1 In international competitive events;

18.2.2 In IBF sanctioned events; and

18.2.3 In other matches (unless the national organization has previously published a decision not to allow such an interval).

18.3   When necessitated by circumstances outside the control of the players, the umpire may suspend play for such a period as the umpire deems necessary. If play is suspended, the existing score shall stand and play is resumed from the point of suspension.

18.4   Under no circumstances shall play be suspended to enable a player to recover his strength or wind, or to receive instruction or advice.

18.5.1 Except in the intervals provided in Laws 18.2 and 18.3, no player shall be permitted to receive advice during a match.

18.5.2 Except at the conclusion of a match, no player shall leave the court without the umpire's consent.

18.6   The umpire shall be the sole judge of suspension of play.

18.7   A player shall not:

18.7.1 Deliberately cause suspension of play;

18.7.2 Deliberately interfere with the speed of the shuttle;

18.7.3 Behave in an offensive manner; or

18.7.4 Be guilty of misconduct not otherwise covered by the Laws of Badminton.

18.8   The umpire shall administer any breach of Laws 18.4, 18.5, or 18.7 by:

18.8.1 Issuing a warning to the offending side;

18.8.2 Faulting the offending side, if previously warned; or

18.8.3 In cases of flagrant or persistent offenses, faulting the offending side and reporting them to the referee, who shall have the power to disqualify.

18.9 When a referee has not been appointed, the responsible official shall have the power to disqualify.

19. Officials and Appeals

19.1 The referee is in overall charge of the tournament or event of which a match forms part.

19.2 The umpire, where appointed, is in charge of the match, the court, and its immediate surroundings. The umpire shall report to the referee. In the absence of a referee, the umpire shall report to the responsible official.

19.3 The service judge shall call any service faults made by the server (Law 11).

19.4 A line judge shall indicate whether a shuttle is in or out.

An Umpire Shall:

19.5 Uphold and enforce the Laws of Badminton and calls faults and lets, should either occur, without appeal being made by the players;

19.6 Give a decision on any appeal regarding a point of dispute, if made before the next service is delivered;

19.7 Ensure that players and spectators are kept informed of the progress of the match;

19.8 Appoint or remove line judges and/or a service judge in consultation with the referee;

19.9 Not overrule the decisions of line judges and the service judge on points of fact;

19.10.1 Where other court officials are not appointed, arrange for their duties to be carried out;

19.10.2 Where an appointed official is unsighted, carry out the official's duties or play a let;

19.11 Decide upon any suspension of play;

19.12 Record and report to the referee all matters in relation to Law 18; and

19.13 Take to the referee all unsatisfied appeals on questions of law only. Such appeals must be made before the next service is delivered, or, if at the end of a game, before the side that appeals has left the court.

YOU BE THE JUDGE

Let's see how much you learned. Here are ten questions about the rules of badminton that cut to the heart of the matter.

1. A player strikes a shuttle that obviously will not clear the net. The striker's opponent, not realizing that the shuttle will be short, takes a swing at it, misses, but hits the net tape with his racket. At the moment the opponent touches the net, the shuttle is about an inch below the top of the net. What's the call?
   a. Nothing.
   b. Call a fault on the opponent for touching the net.
   c. Award the rally to the opponent who touched the net.
   d. Call a let.
2. A player strikes a shuttle that hits the top of the net and begins to fall on the striker's side of the net. The striker's opponent, not realizing that the shuttle has failed to clear the net, swings at it. She misses the shuttle but hits the net with her racket. At the time the opponent touches the net, the shuttle is below tape level on the striker's side of the net. What's the call?
   a. Nothing.
   b. Call a fault on the opponent for touching the net.
   c. Award the rally to the opponent who touched the net.
   d. Call a let.
3. In a doubles match, a player swings at and misses the shuttle. His swing carries his racket head over the net into his opponents' court space. Before the shuttle hits the floor behind him, his partner swats it over the net for an apparent winner. What's the call?
4. A rally ends with the shuttle hitting the chest of a player standing out of bounds. What's the call?
   a. Award the rally to the team striking the shuttle.

    b. Award the rally to the defending team.

    c. Award two points to the striking team—one for winning the rally and another for hitting an opponent in the chest.

    d. Call a let and issue a warning to the defending player for leaving the court.

    e. Call a let and issue a warning to the striking team for hitting an opponent.

5. During a fast-paced rally, a player, not realizing the shuttle will land well out of bounds, drives the bird down her right sideline. It travels below net level to the right of the net pole and lands in the back corner of the opponent's court. What's the call?

    a. Award the rally to the striking player.

    b. Award the rally to the defending player.

    c. Call a let.

6. It's the third game of a doubles match, with Team A leading 14–7 and serving for the match. The partner of the server has a severely sprained ankle but does not want to forfeit the match. As the server prepares to serve, her injured partner sits down on her side of the court near the net. After the serve is delivered, the injured player drags herself just beyond the court's sideline so that she will not interfere with her partner's play. The partner, effectively playing singles against a doubles team, wins the rally. What's the call?

    a. Award the rally and match to the serving team.

    b. Award the rally to the receiving team, because the injured player left the court without permission.

    c. Call a let.

    d. Issue a warning to the injured player for leaving the court without permission.

7. In a doubles match, the "odd" player from Team A delivers a serve from the "even" court. Team A wins the rally. Before the next serve is delivered, the mistake is discovered. What's the call?

    a. Award the rally to Team A.

    b. Award the rally to Team B and issue a warning to Team A for the service error.

    c. Announce that Team A loses its first serve because of

the error. Announce the score followed by "second server."

   d. Announce the service court error of Team A and replay the rally with the "even" player serving for Team A.

8. In a doubles match, the first server from Team B serves and wins three straight rallies. As she is about to serve her fourth in a row, the official realizes that the wrong player on Team B started the serving sequence—that is, the "odd" player started the sequence of serves in the "even" court. What's the call?

   a. Announce that Team B began the serving sequence with a service court error but that the error should not be corrected.

   b. Announce that Team B began the serving sequence with a service court error and that they should correct the error before delivering the next serve.

   c. Announce that Team B must forfeit the previous three points due to the error.

   d. Tell Team B it must forfeit its first serve. Announce the score, followed by "second server."

9. A player hits a shuttle that appears to be headed for the striker's side of the net tape. As the shuttle approaches the top of the net, an earthquake rattles the gym, causing the shuttle to tumble over the net for an apparent winner. What's the call?

   a. Award the rally to the striker.

   b. Award the rally to the striker's opponent.

   c. Call a let.

   d. Flip a coin.

10. At the conclusion of a rally, a player falls to the court, clutching her calf muscle. What's the call?

   a. Ask the injured player if she can continue play.

   b. Call the injured player's coach onto the court.

   c. Tell the injured player to get up and play.

   d. Call an "injury" timeout.

   e. Begin to "count out" the injured player, as in a boxing match. If she does not rise by a count of ten, award the match to the opponent.

Answers:

1. b. According to Law 15.6.1, if a shuttle is in play, it is a fault for one of the players to touch the net. Since the shuttle had not yet touched either floor or net before the player's racket touched the net, it is still in play, even though it would not have cleared the net. The player who touched the net should be faulted.

2. c. The shuttle is not in play if it strikes the net and begins its descent on the striker's side of the net (Law 17.2). In this scenario, the shuttle is not in play by the time the opponent hits the net with her racket. Thus the rally was over before the opponent hit the net and should be awarded to the opponent.

3. It is a fault if a player invades the opponent's air space with a racket (Law 15.6.2), with the following exception: "The striker may, however, follow the shuttle over the net with the racket in the course of a stroke" (Law 15.5). Since the player missed the shuttle, his racket cannot follow the shuttle over the net. A player must strike the shuttle for his follow-through over the net to be ignored.

4. a. The rally should be awarded to the team striking the shuttle. According to Law 15.4.5, it is a fault once the shuttle hits a player, whether the player is on or off the playing surface.

5. a. Award the rally to the player striking the shuttle. The only time the shuttle is required to pass directly over the net is during service (Law 11.1.6). During a rally, the shuttle may legally travel over the net or at any height around the net pole. It is a fault if the shuttle travels under or through the net (Law 15.4.2).

6. a. Award the rally and match to the serving team. The injured player is allowed to take any position on her half of the court that does not prevent the opposing receiver from seeing the shuttle during service (Law 11.5). During the rally, the injured player may crawl off the playing surface to avoid interference with her partner. Although Law 18.5.2 states that players are not allowed to leave the court without the official's permis-

sion, the "court" is defined as the playing surface of the court and its immediate surroundings. A player would not be allowed to crawl into the stands while her partner continued the rally.

7. d. When a service court error is discovered before the next serve is delivered, the error should be corrected and the point replayed only if the team committing the error wins the previous rally.

If the team making the error loses the rally, the error is not corrected. In this case, if Team A had lost the rally, the second server, who was originally the "even" server, would deliver the next serve from the "odd" court (Laws 14.2.1 and 14.4).

8. a. A service court error should be corrected only when both of the following conditions occur: 1) The offending team wins the rally (Law 14.2.1); and 2) the error is detected before the next serve is delivered (Law 14.2.2). In this case, the offending team won the rally after committing the service court error, but the error was discovered too late. It is not corrected, and the "odd" player becomes the "even" player.

9. c. Because the earthquake occurred while the shuttle was still in play (it had not yet hit the net), call a let and suspend the match until it appears safe to play, which may be another day.

10. a. The first step is to ask the injured player if she can continue. The player should be allowed a few seconds to test the severity of the injury and regain her composure. If she indicates she can continue, the match should be resumed immediately.

If the player does not immediately resume play, the official should begin the following sequence of actions:

1) Issue a warning to the injured player for violating Law 18.1 (play shall be continuous), and again ask if she is able to play;

2) fault the injured player for any further delay and again ask if she can continue;

3) if the delay continues, disqualify the injured player.

If a player is injured in an official match, keep the following points in mind. First, play is continuous (Law 18.1), and there is no such thing as an injury timeout. Second, only the injured player can decide if she can continue; no one can order her to play. Third, no one is allowed on the court except players, officials, and medics.

GLOSSARY

ace: A point scored in which the losing player fails to touch the shuttle with his or her racket.

alley: The area between the singles sideline and the doubles sideline.

back alley: The area between the back boundary line and the long service line in doubles. The shuttle may not be served into this area in doubles play.

backcourt: Technically, the back half of the court, though it has come to mean the general area near the back boundary line.

backhand: A stroke played on the left side of a right-handed player, or vice versa.

backswing: The part of the swing in which the player takes the racket back in preparation for the forward swing.

balk: Deceptive movement that disconcerts an opposing player before or during service. Also called a *feint*.

base camp: The spot on the court—centerline, slightly closer to the net than the baseline—to which a singles player should return after most shots. Also called the *center* or *basic position*.

baselines: The boundary lines farthest from the net.

bird: Slang term for *shuttlecock*.

block: To hit the shuttle with a stationary racket, causing it to rebound to the opponent's side of the net.

carry: To hold, however briefly, the shuttle on the racket during a stroke; a fault.

clear: A high, deep lob designed to go over the opponent's head and clear him or her from the net.

court: The area of play bounded by the outer lines of play. Although badminton rules and regulations were drawn up and published as early as 1877, the variety of interpretations of court size and shape delayed the development of the game well into the twentieth century.

cross-court: A shot that sends the shuttle diagonally from one side of the net to the other.

deception: The art of camouflaging one's intent in order to make different shots look the same.

defense: The position you are in when you are on the run and cannot use placements to open the court to your advantage.

diagonal: One of the four basic

ways to position players in doubles play, with each player covering a triangular area of the court.

double hit: A stroke in which the racket hits the shuttle twice in succession.

doubles: A version of the game in which two players are on each side of the net.

drive: A hard, flat-trajectory shot that travels low over the net.

driven clear: A clear shot that has a rather flat trajectory as it passes over an opponent's head.

driven serve: A hard-hit serve with a flat trajectory.

drop shot: A finesse stroke hit with little speed that falls close to the net on the opponent's side.

face: The stringed hitting surface of the racket.

fault: A service or return that is illegal, that fails to clear the net, or that lands out of bounds.

feint: Deceptive movement that disconcerts a player before or during service. Also called a *balk*.

flick: A quick movement of the wrist, with little arm movement, that can send the shuttle high and deep.

flick serve: A serve delivered with the motion described above.

follow-through: The smooth, continuous path of the racket after it has contacted the shuttle; an essential part of the swing.

foot fault: Illegal movement of the feet or stepping on the service line during service.

forecourt: The part of each side of the court closest to the net.

forehand: A stroke played on the right side of a right-handed player, or vice versa.

front-and-back: One of the four basic ways to position players in doubles play. Also called *up-and-back*.

front service line: The line parallel to, and 6 $1/2$ feet from, the net on each side of the court, forming the forward boundary of the service courts.

game bird: The point that will enable the server to win the game.

hairpin net shot: Stroke made from below and very close to the net, with the shuttle just clearing the net and dropping sharply downward; takes its name from the arc of the shuttle in a well-executed shot.

half-court shot: A shot placed midcourt; especially effective against a doubles team in the front-and-back formation.

handicap: A point advantage given to the weaker side when sides are not evenly matched

hand-out: Loss of service by the serving team. Also called side-out.

head: The oval end of the racket.

high clear: A clear shot that rises high in the air and drops near an opponent's back line.

International Badminton Federation (IBF): The world governing body of the sport, established in 1934. One of its many duties is the management of international team competitions known as the Thomas Cup (men) and Uber Cup (women).

inning: The period during which the serving team holds service.

in side: The side serving (to the out side).

kill: Fast downward shot that usually cannot be returned. Also called a *put-away.*

let: Any exchange or rally that is replayed.

lob: A high shot that goes over the opponent's head.

long serve: A serve hit deep in the service court.

long service line: The rear boundary line in singles.

love: No score, or zero. A score of 2–love, for example, would mean the server has two, the opponent zero.

match: Best two out of three games.

match point: The point that, if won by the server, wins the match for him or her.

midcourt: The center of the court, approximately halfway between the net and the back line.

mixed doubles: A version of doubles badminton in which male and female play as teammates.

net shot: Shot hit from the forecourt in which the shuttle just clears the net. Popular net shots include hairpin net shots, push shots, and net smashes.

New York Badminton Club (NYBC): Founded in 1878, the NYBC claims to be the oldest organized badminton club in the world.

obstruction: Hindrance of a player making a shot.

offense: The attacking side.

out: A shuttle that lands outside a boundary line is said to be out.

open up court: To put an opponent on the defensive, moving him around so that he cannot cover the whole court.

out-of-hand: A type of serve in which the shuttle is held in the hand until just before the racket contacts it.

out side: The side receiving serve (from the in side).

pass: To hit the shuttle to the side of and out of reach of an opponent.

passing shot: A shot that goes past an opponent.

placement: Hitting the shuttle to advantageous spots on the court.

push shot: A gentle net shot played by pushing the shuttle without great force.

put-away: Fast downward shot that usually cannot be returned. Also called a *kill*.

rally: A series of consecutive returns back and forth across the net in a game or warmup.

ready position: An alert body position—facing the net, weight evenly distributed on the balls of both feet, racket poised—that enables a player to move quickly in any direction.

rotation: One of the four basic ways to position players in doubles. Both players rotate counterclockwise as play demands. Also called *combination*.

round-the head shot: An overhead stroke played on the left side of the body, so that the contact point is above the left shoulder.

rush the serve: Quick sprint to the net in an attempt to put away a short, low serve by smashing the shuttle down into the opponent's court; used mainly in doubles.

second service: A term normally used in doubles to indicate that one partner has already had a turn serving.

serve: The act of putting the shuttle in play; opening stroke of each rally. Also called *service*.

service court: The area into which the serve must be delivered.

setting: Changing the number of points needed to win a game; done by rule at certain tie scores.

setup: A poor shot that leaves a kill for the opponent.

shaft: The part of the racket between the head and the handle.

short: A shot that fails to reach its mark, such as a serve that falls in front of the proper service court.

short serve: A serve hit shallow in the service court.

shuttle: The feathered friend of badminton players. Also called *shuttlecock* or *bird*.

side-by-side: A doubles formation in which both players occupy positions approximately equidistant from the net.

side in: The side whose turn it is to serve.

side-out: When the serving side loses the serve to the receiving side.

singles game: A game in which there are two players, one on each side of the court.

sling: A shot in which the shuttle is carried forward on the racket; a fault. Also called a *throw*.

smash: A hard-hit overhead shot that forces the shuttle sharply downward; the chief attacking stroke.

stroke: The act of striking the shuttle with the racket.

toss serve: A type of serve in which the server tosses the shuttle prior to contact.

United States Badminton Association (USBA): The national governing body of badminton in the United States.

volley: To hit the shuttle in the air before it touches the ground; hence, all legal badminton shots are volleys.

wood shot: A shot in which the shuttle contacts the frame, throat, shaft, or handle of the racket instead of the strings. Although it's a bad shot, the IBF ruled in 1963 that a wood shot is legal.

RESOURCES

CLUBS

If you want to become more seriously involved in badminton, start hanging out with people who share your enthusiasm for the sport. In other words, join a club. There are five main ways to go about it.

1. Start your own club. Home-based clubs typically have a one- or two-family core, with neighbors or other family members added as their interest grows.
2. Join a private badminton club. This is typically an organized group of ten to one hundred members, usually adults who enjoy both the competitive and the social benefits of the game.
3. Join a country club, tennis club, or sports club that, although dominated by other sports, offers badminton to its members.
4. Attend a school or college that has a club or team. Many schools offer badminton on both an intramural and interschool level.
5. Join a retirement community that offers badminton.

The United States Badminton Association (USBA) oversees all serious badminton competition in the United States. Benefits of USBA membership include the following:

- Subscription to the quarterly magazine *Badminton USA.*
- Subscription to the newsletter *Badminton News.*
- Ratings and rankings. This is the way grassroots players can know how they compare with other players.
- Rebates to regions. Twenty percent of the USBA dues are rebated to regional organizations to support local development of the sport.
- Liability insurance.
- National championships. There are now six national championships nationally, from the junior to the senior level.
- Service from the USBA national office. Questions are courteously answered.
- Tournaments. More than 120 USBA-sanctioned tournaments are held, many of them for grassroots players.

Peruse the following list of clubs registered with the United States Badminton Association to determine if any are in your neighborhood.

To learn more about clubs, to update information, or to receive organizational assistance, contact the United States Badminton Association (USBA), One Olympic Plaza, Colorado Springs, CO 80909, telephone 719-578-4808, fax 719-578-4507. The executive director is Jim Hadley, but other members of the staff can help you and are friendly and informative.

The USBA also can provide instructional materials, information on educational clinics, tournament formats, player ratings, national championships, and subscriptions to *Badminton USA* and *Badminton News*. These benefits easily justify the nominal dues.

THE USBA MEMBER-CLUB DIRECTORY

CALIFORNIA

Badminton Club of Leisure World, 706 C Sevilla, Laguna Hills, CA 92653, 714-458-2696.

Cal State–Sacramento Badminton, Cal State–Sacramento, 600 J St., Dept. of Physical Education, Sacramento, CA 95819.

Camden Badminton Club, 3369 Union Ave., San Jose, CA 95124, 408-559-8553.

Cypress High School Badminton Club, 3916 Maxson Rd., #B, El Monte, CA 91732, 818-579-2345.

East LA College Badminton, 1301 Avenida Cesar Chavez, Monterey Park, CA 91104, 213-265-8917.

Foothill Badminton Club, 3121 Ross Rd., Palo Alto, CA 94303, 415-493-1039.

Franklin High School Badminton Club, 1210 Mac Duff, Stockton, CA 95209, 209-944-4475.

Garden Grove High School Club, 11271 Stamford Ave., Garden Grove, CA 92640, 714-663-6183.

Lake County Badminton Club, 7803 Wight Way, Kelseyville, CA 95451, 707-279-2616.

Manhattan Beach Badminton Club, 664 18th St., Manhattan Beach, CA, 310-545-9052.

Mendocino Badminton Club, 14199 Hanson Circle, Mendocino, CA 95460, 707-964-4347.

Pasadena Badminton Club, 17002 Cotter Place, Encino, CA 91436, 805-372-8142.

Peninsula Badminton Club, 757-A Calderon Ave., Mountain View, CA 94041, 415-961-2865.

San Diego Badminton Club, 3121 "D" Evening Way, La Jolla, CA 92037, 619-457-1999.

Santa Ana High School Badminton Club, 41 Calle Del Sur, Rancho Santa Margarita, CA 92688, 714-567-4978.

Seahawk Badminton Club, 16022 Waltz Circle, Huntington Beach, CA 92649, 714-840-0767.

Stanford Badminton Club, Stanford University, Dept. of Athletics, Roble Gym, Stanford, CA 94305, 415-497-6352.

Sunnyvale Badminton Club, 839 Pagoda Tree Court, Sunnyvale, CA 94086, 408-256-6168.

U.C. Berkeley, U.C. Berkeley Sports Club Program, 2301 Bancroft Way, Berkeley, CA 94720, 510-547-6426.

U.C. Davis Badminton Club, University of California–Davis, 140 Recreation Hall, Davis, CA 95616.

COLORADO

Denver Athletic Club–Badminton, 1325 Glenarm Place, Denver, CO 80204, 303 534-1211.

Mile High Badminton Club, 1036 W. 8th Ave., Denver, CO 80204, 303-534-6789.

Pikes Peak Badminton Club, 2104 N. Tejon St., Colorado Springs, CO 90807, 719-635-4088.

CONNECTICUT

Boys' and Girls' Club of Greenwich, 4 Horseneck Lane, Greenwich,CT 06830, 203-869-3224.

Greenwich Badminton Club, 39 Jones Park, Riverside, CT 06878, 203-637-2623.

Lyme–Old Lyme Middle School, Lyme St., Old Lyme, CT 06371, 203-434-2568.

Pinewood Lake Trumbull Badminton, 16 Hemlock Trail, Trumbull, CT 06611, 203-306-7221.

Return of Serve Badminton Club, 60 Main St., Farmington, CT 06032, 203-677-1321.

The Badminton Club of New Haven, 7 Ridgewood Terrace, New Haven, CT 06473, 203-795-4453.

West Hartford Badminton Club, 12 Byron Rd., Granby, CT 06035, 203-653-7398.

DISTRICT OF COLUMBIA

GWU Badminton Club, 817 23rd St. NW, Washington, DC 20052, 202-994-7112.

Howard University Badminton Club, Dept. of Physical Education, Howard University, Washington, DC 20059, 202-806-6681.

Pentagon Athletic Club, Room BG 877 Army, The Pentagon, Washington, DC 20310, 703-521-8044.

FLORIDA

Miami Badminton Club, 11172 SW 25th St., Miami, FL 33165, 305-556-4235.

GEORGIA

Atlanta Athletic Club Badminton Club, Bobby Jones Dr., Duluth, GA 30136, 404-448-1366.

Georgia State University Badminton Club, English Dept., Georgia State University, University Plaza, Decatur, GA 30030, 404-651-2904.

HAWAII

Hilo Badminton Club, 2072 Kinoole, Hilo, HI 96720, 808-935-2821.

ILLINOIS

Chi-Town Badminton Club, 6506 Deer Lane, Palos Heights, IL 60463, 708-371-8788.

Forest View Badminton Club, 1124 Valleystream Dr., Wheeling, IL 60090, 708-541-5335.

IBIS, 504 E. White #23, Champaign, IL 61820, 217-352-7454.

McKinley Park Badminton Club, 2902 West 39th Place, Chicago, IL 60632, 312-523-1534.

Park Ridge Badminton Club, 316 S. Hilusi, Mount Prospect, IL 60056.

SIUC Badminton Club, Student Recreation Center, Carbondale, IL 62901.

University of Chicago Badminton Club, 5125 S. Ellis Ave., Chicago, IL 60615, 312-702-6945.

Victor Sports, P.O. Box 208, Hinsdale, IL 60522, 708-352-1580.

INDIANA

Race Badminton Club, 5122 Jensen Rd., Martinsville, IN 46151, 317-349-1308.

KENTUCKY

Louisville Badminton Club, 3819 Ashridge Dr., Louisville, KY 40241, 502-426-3219.

LOUISIANA

New Orleans Badminton Club, 4846 Camp St., New Orleans, LA 70115, 504-865-2480.

Shreveport Badminton Club, P.O. Box 1527, Shreveport, LA 71165, 318-869-2073.

MAINE

Tennis of Maine, Inc., 196 U.S. Route 1, Falmouth, ME 04105, 207-781-2671.

MARYLAND

Badminton Club of Washington, DC, 5815 Greenlawn Dr., Bethesda, MD 20814, 301-345-1383.

MASSACHUSETTS

Bird and Bottle Club, P.O. Box 61P, South Dartmouth, MA 02748, 508-997-1515.

City of Wells Badminton Club, P.O. Box 1528, Vineyard Haven, MA 02568, 508-693-0829.

Maugus Club, 40 Abbott Rd., Wellesley Hills, MA 02181, 617-235-9805.

MICHIGAN

Birmingham Badminton Club, 28925 Millbrook Rd., Farmington, MI 48334, 810-544-8010.

Dearborn Westwood Badminton Club, 2010 Hollywood, Dearborn, MI 48124, 313-336-5959.

Grosse Point Badminton Association, 409 Chalfonte, Grosse Point Farms, MI 48236, 313-885-8232.

Lake Michigan College Badminton Club, 315 Pearl St., South Haven, MI 49090, 616-637-1565.

MINNESOTA

Minneapolis Athletic Club, 615 Second Ave. S., Minneapolis, MN 55402, 612-339-3655.

MISSOURI

Gateway Badminton Club, 4514 Pegasus Dr., St. Louis, MO 63129, 314-487-7187.

St. Louis Badminton Club, 8884 Woodpark Dr., St. Louis, MO 63127, 314-843-3660.

NEBRASKA

Top Flight Badminton Club, 406 Circle Dr., Papillion, NE 68046, 402-592-7309.

NEW JERSEY

Mountain Lakes Badminton Club, 5 Basswood Dr., Denville, NJ 07834, 201-625-2134.

NEW MEXICO

Mesilla Valley Badminton Club, 1502 N. Tornillo St., Las Cruces, NM 88001, 505-524-4265.

NEW YORK

Amherst Recreation Badminton Club, 187 Delamere Rd., Williamsville, NY 14221, 716-634-5248.

Badminton Club of Greater Buffalo, 228 Louvaine Dr., Buffalo, NY 14223, 716-873-9800.

Badminton Club of New York, 103 East 84th St., New York, NY 10028, 212-535-1609.

Brooklyn Badminton Club, Dept. of P.E., Brooklyn College, Bedford and Avenue H, Brooklyn, NY 11210, 718-951-5879.

Central Manhattan Badminton Club, 402 E. 90th St., #7B, New York, NY 10128, 212-831-0302.

Garden City Badminton Club, 79 North Saint Pauls Rd., Hempstead, NY 11550, 516-483-8185.

Miller Place Badminton Club, P.O. Box 780, Miller Place, NY 11764, 516-473-2723.

Northport Badminton Club, 1014 Fort Salonga Rd., Northport, NY 11768, 516-261-1440.

Queensborough Community College Badminton Club, Dept. HPE & Dance, Queensborough Community College, Bayside, NY 11364, 718-631-6325.

NORTH CAROLINA

Charlotte Badminton Club, 510 East Park Ave., Charlotte, NC 28203, 704-892-5680.

OHIO

Shaker Badminton Club, 3005 Coleridge Rd., Cleveland, OH 44118, 216-932-3426.

The College of Wooster Badminton Club, Armington PE Center, Wooster College, Wooster, OH 44691, 216-263-2189.

OKLAHOMA

Conoco Badminton Club, P.O. Box 1267, Ponca City, OK 74601, 405-767-2202.

University of Oklahoma Badminton Club, Dept. of Educational Leadership, University of Oklahoma, Norman, OK 73019, 405-447-8507.

OREGON

Central Oregon Community College, 2600 NW College Way, Bend, OR 97701, 503-383-7794.

Multnomah Athletic Club, P.O. Box 390, Portland, OR 97207, 503-223-8740.

University of Oregon Club Sports Badminton, EMU Club Sports, P.O. Box 3600, University of Oregon, Eugene, OR 97403, 503-346-3733.

PENNSYLVANIA

Albright College Badminton Club, Albright College, P.O. Box 15234, Reading, PA 19612.

Bryn Mawr College Badminton Club, Bryn Mawr College, Dept. of Athletics, Bryn Mawr, PA 19010.

Drexel Badminton Club, 3007 Park Ave., Lafayette Hill, PA 19444, 610-828-4677.

Germantown Cricket Club, 411 Manheim St., Philadelphia, PA 19144.

Kimberton Badminton Club, A227 Westridge Gardens, Phoenixville, PA 19460, 610-933-4939.

Mansfield University Badminton, 214 Belknap Hall, Mansfield University, Mansfield, PA 16933, 717-662-4613.

Swarthmore College Badminton Club, Dept. of Physical Education, 500 College Ave., Swarthmore, PA 19081, 610-328-8218.

The Fitness Business, 238 Corwen Terrace, West Chester, PA 19380, 610-363-5857.

RHODE ISLAND

Block Island Badminton Club, Box 247, Block Island, RI 02807, 401-466-2819.

TENNESSEE

Memphis Badminton Club, 601 S. Goodlett, Memphis TN 38111, 901-452-4579.

TEXAS

Houston Badminton Club, 5514 Linden Court, Spring, TX 77379, 713-370-2091.

North Dallas Badminton Association, 2402 Acacia St., Richardson, TX 75082, 214-907-9801.

San Antonio Badminton Club, 2811 Woodrock, San Antonio, TX 78251, 210-680-4633.

University of Texas at Austin Badminton, Recreational Sports, Gregory 33, Austin, TX 78712, 512-371-0445.

VIRGINIA

Sports Network, 8320 Quarry Rd., Manassas, VA 22110, 703-335-1555.

Virginia Badminton Club, 3713 S. George Mason, #1711 W, Falls Church, VA 22041, 703-578-4085.

WISCONSIN

Greater Milwaukee Badminton Club, 6868 Kathleen Court #2, Franklin, WI 53132, 414-427-8658.

University of Wisconsin Badminton Club, 1509 University Ave., Madison, WI 53706, 608-238-8994.